An Awkward Fit

A powerfully personal account of a young mans struggles to stay alive and live a normal life

I0099813

Helen Maczkowiack

chipmunkapublishing
the mental health publisher

Helen Maczkowiack

Published by
Chipmunkapublishing
PO Box 6872
Brentwood
Essex CM13 1ZT
United Kingdom

http://www.chipmunkapublishing.com

Edited by Marc Wilson

Chipmunkapublishing gratefully acknowledge the support of Arts Council England.

To my grandsons Ryan, Lachlan, Daniel and Matthew. They taught me how to love again when darkness took over my life. To the memory of our son Stephen, who has left a legacy through his writings. He desperately wanted to be understood, and through his memoirs in this book he achieved it.

And to all those who feel as if they don't fit into this world, to let them know they are not alone with these same feelings as our son had. This world belongs to them also.

Helen Maczkowiack

Contents

Preface

Part 1

Part 2

Part 3

Part 4

Acknowledgements

There are many people I would like to thank for their time,
advice and emotional support, which made this book possible
and who kept me going with their encouragement and input
during those dark times when I thought I could not go on.
I would especially like to thank my husband, Darrel, who
encouraged me to continue when I was overcome with
anxiety and grief. Also, my daughter, Nicky, for her patience
and understanding when the book took priority over her needs.
To my special friend Joy Mildren who coped with my endless
phone calls and cries for help, my heartfelt thanks. And to
Peter Haran who spent endless hours patiently tutoring me in
the art of writing. To Darrell Ingham for his research and help
in wading through the endless paperwork. My thanks to
Heather Britton for her generosity and friendship, a master
with words who knew how I wanted this book to be and
helped me achieve it. To Bronte Price, Sue Tuesner and David
Schubert who did a fantastic job of editing this book.

Thanks also to Stephen's ex-wife who allowed me to write
about her time with him, her only stipulation being that I told
the truth. To Linda and Sally for allowing me to publish their
letters. I would like to thank a number of people who took
time out of their very busy schedules to review the manuscript
and offered helpful comments: Piet Crosby, Heather
Ashmeade, Ingrid Alderton, Alison Thompson, Helen Scales,
Graham Quinton and Sue Ingham. There are others I have
failed to mention who have entered my life in so many
significant ways over the seven years it has taken to complete
this book; my heartfelt thanks to you and all who loved and
cared about Stephen.

Helen Maczkowiack

Preface

An Awkward Fit is the haunting story of a young man's desperate struggles to fit into a world that was different from how he imagined it should be. After many years of anguish, at the age of 29 he ended his life. Stephen was a gifted writer and kept comprehensive accounts of his life from an early age, which I discovered only after his death. His carefully described thoughts, the sensations he experienced and the emotional reactions he recorded became the basis for this book. This has given voice to the silent suffering of many young and not so young people of today.

I was driven to tell this story by a strong desire and determination such as I had never encountered before. Even though I had no previous experience at writing, I knew with deep certainty that the day would come when I would complete the story of our son's desperate struggle to survive in a world of confusion.

I put my thoughts down on paper and into a tape recorder. At times my mind felt as if it was exploding with all the thoughts and ideas on how to write this book. There were many occasions when I became both physically and mentally drained, overcome with anxiety and grief. The biggest mystery for me as I wrote was: Why did this happen? I would have died for him. Why couldn't he live for me? There were times when I wanted to die so I could be with my son. I was suspended between two worlds: One that I no longer wanted to live in without my son, the other that contained my husband, beautiful daughter and my grandsons. There was no turning back – this book had become my motivation for living. I had to complete the task I set for myself.

My primary motivation was to preserve our son's writings. I wanted this to be something I could do for him, but as I became more and more involved with his story and his words, a secondary goal emerged. This book could be of enormous value in promoting awareness about mental health issues, to support the development of more effective responses from the various community services, those who work with people who are experiencing the same difficulties that Stephen faced.

I have tried to tell Stephen's story as honestly as I can, without offending or hurting people in any way. If I have, then I have not done it deliberately. I have simply told the story as I see it and from the information supplied by others, or as Stephen wrote it in his memoirs. In some instances it has been necessary to change people's names to protect their privacy.

An Awkward Fit

Well, when I sat down to write these following words they just came to me. I do hope that at least some of the words become inscribed in your mind that you may know to some extent what sort of person I, Stephen Maczkowiack, was.

I love my family first, and then I love everyone! I pity those who don't love everyone! ... We're all afraid of the dark but morning always comes. I see the sun and I smile. My heart, my soul, my thoughts I searched, to make some sense of it all. It seems to me according to my eyes and ears that nothing is right, nothing is wrong – it just is. Passion writes these words and love is its strength. If only success gave me the opportunity to exercise this strength. My love does not die; it just finds a new home. Now, because you read these words, the love inside me lives on in you!

The book consists of my son's writings as well as my own, most of his writings are at the beginning of each chapter followed by my own narratives and to distinguish between the two writers my son's writing is in bold

Helen Maczkowiack

Part 1

CHAPTER 1 – 1998 -A Knock at the Door

I can't take it any more; why can't I forget the hurt? When does the hurt stop? It's just too hard to live with. I can't stand being alone; no one ever stays this unhappy. Something that's a part of me is lost; things that I love always go away. My heart is truly heavy, almost physical. I'm sad. Please let me die, should tomorrow be sad! Who will grow old and be happy with me?

~

August 1998, 3.45 pm. I came home from work and had my usual cup of coffee. It was now 20 past four and I was peeling the last carrot for our evening meal. Darrel finished work at 5pm and would be home at five past six.

Someone was knocking on the front door; I put the carrot down and rinsed my hands at the kitchen sink. I opened the door to a police officer.

'Is this the home of Stephen Maczkowiack?'

'Yes,' I looked blankly at him, not daring to wonder why he was here.

The few seconds of silence between us felt endless. Nathan, our neighbour's son who had been playing with Lego on the kitchen floor, nuzzled in beside me.

'Please go home,' I whispered to him.

Turning back to the officer, I said,' I'm Stephen's mother. Do you want to come in?' I held the screen door open as he brushed past me into the front porch, and ushered him into the kitchen.

My mind was spinning, apprehension and uneasiness sweeping over me.

Why is he here? I had trained myself, over the years, not to get excited, but to stay calm and deal with whatever situation

Stephen was in. The officer's exact words from that point on now escape me, but the essence of them will remain with me all my days: 'Your son was found in his unit in Barmera at four o'clock this afternoon. He hanged himself.'

I remember the word 'hanged' clearly. It echoed through my head and ricocheted through my whole body. Time stood still.

'No! No way! That's not true!' I screamed back at him. My brain felt like it was exploding from overload of what had just been said, at the same time trying to reject it. It was a message from hell.

I grasped at a thought that was completely irrational. *He didn't actually say he was dead.* Maybe … But I knew it was true. The look on the officer's face said it.

I recall my head was dull and empty, my body in shock. I kept shaking my arms; I guess I didn't know what else to do with them. At the same time I willed my legs not to collapse on me. I felt as though a clamp was compressing my stomach and chest, trying to squeeze the last breath out of me. I couldn't even cry 'No!' any more. All I could do was make a pitiful cry like some injured animal, and the noise kept coming over and over again. I was marching around the room, still shaking my arms like a demented wind-up toy.

I have no idea how long I kept this up, but eventually I was aware of the police officer holding me, trying to calm me down. And I remember his saying this was the hardest part of his job. 'I am the same age as your son.'

He rang the station to advise I was so distraught that he would stay with me until my husband came home. I have no recollection of whether I gave him Darrel's work number or if I dialled it for him. *Why did this happen? What went wrong?* We had been with him five days ago in Barmera and he had looked happier than I'd seen him for a long time. He was in good spirits. In fact Darrel had said, as we drove away that night, 'I think he's going to be fine.'

An Awkward Fit

There were two reasons we had gone to visit Stephen; he wanted us to see where he lived and worked, and we were also concerned for his general wellbeing. He was working five days a week installing irrigation systems and fruit picking on weekends. He only had every third weekend off, when he would return to his home in Gawler to see his friends and work on his garden. He didn't seem to be able to stop working. He had been through five very difficult years.

The break-up of his marriage, a work injury that prevented him from getting a job and having to cope with constant pain were only some of the difficulties that had caused his loss of confidence in himself and his ability to succeed in life. And then things seemed to be looking up – he was no longer heavily in debt and he had a job. However, we were concerned about him living alone because he suffered from depression and we still had a lingering uneasiness, although this was laid to rest, to some degree, after our visit.

While waiting for Darrel to have a shower before we headed home to Craigmore, Stephen and I squatted together in front of his unit, on that last evening we had together.
'I shouldn't smoke,' said Stephen, reaching into the top pocket of his shirt for his cigarettes.' Dad wouldn't like it.'
Given all that Stephen had been through, and his fragile state, smoking seemed a minor transgression. I told him if he wanted to smoke to go ahead, it was all right with me. He leaned back against the wall and gave a contented sigh.
'Look at that,' he said, waving his arm to indicate the beautiful sunset across the lake.' Who else do you know who's lucky enough to come home from work and see this view every night?'
This was a rare and magical moment for us both. It was truly magnificent.

Later that week at home in Adelaide, I tried to contact Stephen to let him know someone was interested in seeing his résumé. I had seen a job I thought would suit him advertised in the paper, and mentioned this to Stephen when we were in Barmera the weekend before. It was for an irrigation firm that was looking for someone with experience. Stephen expressed interest and said I could phone them. The person I spoke to understood that he was tied to his current job until November but said he should still send his résumé. Stephen didn't have a phone in his unit so I rang his work, but he hadn't turned up for two days. I wasn't overly concerned and thought perhaps he was sick. He wasn't sick – he was dead.

Now he's gone ... and there are so many unanswered questions.
My life had changed forever. I could no longer look outside and appreciate the gum trees or the daffodils and the lavender that grew in my small backyard garden. I looked at the statue of Bambi with its ear missing. It was the same as yesterday; nothing had changed, except me. How I hated being me. I loathed everything about life. I felt nothing but wretchedness.
How could I survive? How could I get through this and keep on living? I wanted to die. It was a fight to survive each day, a fight to want to live more than I wanted to die. I wanted so desperately to reach out and drag our son back to life.
When I cleared out his flat I felt like an intruder going through his possessions. It was as though we were eliminating any evidence of his existence. However, I made an amazing discovery. Packed neatly in a box I found copious notes and journals, and the early stages of a book he had begun to write about his life. I had no idea it existed.
I began reading. I hadn't realised how confused Stephen was, or how deeply troubled. These diaries were the key that would ultimately open the door for me, giving me a better insight into who he was, how he felt, giving me entrée into his soul. They were the entry point to so many of my unanswered questions.
When I read his words, as I have done many times, I almost feel that I *am* Stephen. I imagine myself sitting in front of the

boxes doing those things he wrote about. My mind becomes his, and it's as if he is alive in me. I can see him now, sitting cross-legged on the floor dressed in black jeans and tank top, his lean shoulders slightly hunched over, his hair dishevelled and hanging on his shoulders, his eyes alert and his face transfixed as he reaches into one of the boxes.

I can't keep my anguish from surfacing. The tears make it difficult for me to read, but I must. I want to understand him. I want to try to find out why this happened. He seemed to journey into dimensions where most of us wouldn't even attempt to go.

It's five minutes past 2 am, 14 April 1969. The place is the maternity ward of the Queen Victoria Hospital and I am holding my just-born son. He weighed 7 pounds 13 ounces, with beautiful smooth skin and he was not nearly as red and wrinkly as I thought he would be. I'm seeing him through a blur of tears. His tiny face, so perfect, little hands clenched into fists. I'm a mother. I've gone through the pain; I am still going through it from the tear I received when he entered the world. It's worth it – I'd do it all again.

Stephen was a crying baby from when he first entered the world. The only time he seemed to be settled was when he was feeding and for about an hour afterwards. I recall now those first days and how that unrelenting cry upset me. I also recall the squeak of Darrel's army boots on the lino-covered passageways of the hospital that told me he was coming to visit us. I remember him entering the hospital ward with everyone watching the door to see who had squeaky boots on – and to see the man with his jumper inside out.

Childbirth – staring out the maternity ward window, I realised that the birth of Stephen had been much more than childbirth – I had stepped from the world of a nineteen-year-old teenager into adulthood. *I feel excited, I'm not a child of a family, any more. I'm a mother! I have my own child, my own family.*

Before the Queen Vic, a ten-storey structure overlooking Adelaide's Victoria Park Racecourse, my world was fruit orchards astride the sand filled paddocks and hills of the upper Murray Mallee country.

The town was Loxton in the late 1960s and it was in this, my hometown, I met my future husband, Darrel.

Darrel worked at the Loxton Co-op hardware store when we first got married, a salesman selling fertiliser, irrigation supplies and pesticides. But his father and uncle pestered him to take on an apprenticeship 'to secure his future' and to keep the oldies happy. Darrel relented and sat for an exam for a position as a PMG trainee linesman.

He didn't think he had a chance at the job – there were more than 600 applicants and they only wanted about 25.

Darrel's heart wasn't in moving. His life has always been in the Riverland, the family, the friendships made, fishing and shooting – the 21-yearold was happy to keep his roots firmly in Loxton. Several weeks later, a letter arrived, offering a traineeship as a linesman in Adelaide.

Freedom.

I wanted out of Loxton. I wanted away from the river, away from the monotony and exhaustion of the fruit blocks. *I wanted a life.*

It was the summer of 1969, I was three months pregnant and the move from Loxton had exhausted me.

The place now was the front porch of Grandma Mabel's 19th-century cottage in Vernon St, Norwood – our temporary home for the next twelve months.

Grandma Mabel Dawson's life was the pensioners' club, the front porch in her favourite chair knitting, peeling the same three vegies at the old kitchen sink each night and the ever-present diabetic odour in the toilet and bathroom.

Queen Victoria Hospital was a 20-minute bus ride from Vernon Street and 45 minutes walking back for my fortnightly check-ups. It was a weekday morning in the maternity hospital, waiting in the reception area along with a dozen women, arms folded over bulging stomachs and the occasional nurse, starched and supercilious.

I didn't laugh or even smile when the duty nurse stood in the doorway of the examination room. My mother had come from Loxton to be with me.

The nurse called :'Mrs Mak-a-waky?'

'That you?' I turned, to the sight of my mother plopped in the chair next to me, doubled over, laughing. She laughed and laughed and I joined her, with tears rolling down our faces.

The nurse resembled Broom Hilda or at the least her twin, with her rounded figure and skinny short legs and eyes and nose that were too big for her small peaky face. She failed to get the joke. Mum was still laughing when I came back from my check-up.

I was totally exhausted for the last months of my pregnancy. When Darrel went to work, I'd lie down almost unconscious until he returned in the evening. The only daily interruption to my comatose state was when the baker banged on the door. With a whispered *shit,* I swung from the bed and stumbled to the door, wrenching it open.

'You've woken me up again!'

I flung the bread on the kitchen table and retreated back to the darkened bedroom. Back to bed under the covers, munching on a sticky, warm freshly-baked currant bun.

Two days after the birth of Stephen I was feeling quite fit, and anxious to take him home. A nurse pushing a trolley hovers at my bedside. She picks up a steel funnel and some other smaller objects. She smiles, with 'We need to look inside you.' She draws the curtains around my bed. There was a sudden excruciating pain where I had torn during the birth. It felt like the wound that was beginning to knit together had been wrenched apart.

'Shit!' I screamed.

'There, it's nearly over.'

From that point on there was almost unrelenting pain from the tear. What had been an enjoyable experience was now a nightmare and I was in some sort of post-birth shock … I was now extremely frightened and didn't want them to use the funnel again, so I said nothing about my ongoing pain.

I was barely able to walk when I was allowed to go home five days later. Darrel came to collect us. I remember anchoring my feet on the floor of the car and pushing my back into the back rest so that I could keep my bottom raised up from the seat to prevent me from sitting on my stitches, but still looking to every one else as if I was sitting down. I was afraid they would keep me in hospital. I was not only homesick I was also physically ill.

The first days home with my new baby were feeds chundered down my back or spread across his tiny chest, leaving Stephen constantly hungry and crying. He cried for much of the day, and usually all night. I was continually worn out from feeding him, trying to satisfy his hunger. I was up with him all night and it seemed the only time he stopped crying was when I held him. It didn't occur to me that there was any other way I could have handled it but to sit up all night nursing him. I grew fatigued and weaker as an infection raged through my body. If Stephen wasn't crying, then I was.

Darrel started physically holding me down in bed, hoping that I would get some rest. But the more he held me, the more I struggled and cried.

'How much longer can this go on?' Darrel asked.

I ate very little, so cooking was not a priority for me.

'Can't you cook something different? I can't stomach any more of this every night!' Darrel complained, looking at his plate containing a concoction of mincemeat and mashed potato dotted with a few carrots.

I never thought about whether he liked potato pie every night, and cooking was the least of my concerns. I wasn't interested in eating and, besides, I had no idea how to cook.

I glared at him. 'Something wrong with it?'

I discovered that if I boiled mincemeat, thickened it with gravy, added a few carrots and topped it with mashed potatoes and browned it in the oven it made a reasonable meal that Darrel and my brother Trevor, who was now staying with us and serving an apprenticeship under grumpy Uncle Fred, would eat. I didn't realise that my cooking was the reason that Trevor was buying hamburgers and pies every night instead of eating at home, and Darrel was sneaking out to the Norwood pie cart in the early hours of the morning to buy a pie floater.

Darrel suffered in silence, until one night in the second week home he shouted, 'I can't stand this any longer!'

He grabbed Stephen in one of his crying fits and stormed out to the car. Darrel's nightly drives around the city were to become a regular occurrence. We had discovered that Stephen would fall asleep the moment he was in a moving car. But only a short time after the car stopped, he would start crying again. Darrel's state was understandable. He found it increasingly difficult to manage studying until early hours of the morning, together with Stephen constantly crying and looking after a sick wife. He needed help.

He rang his mother at Loxton.

'Mum, we are simply not managing. Can you come down and help for a while?' Ivy, his mother, was working at the time, but she asked for time off from her cleaning duties at the hospital and came to help look after our household.

Grandma Mabel was still living with us, but she suffered from diabetes so was frequently unwell and also in need of care.

Ivy cleaned the house, looked after Stephen and cooked. Still the infection was spreading through my body and I was unaware of the severity of it. I was exhausted, drained of all energy. I was barely capable of feeding Stephen and stayed in bed most of the day while Darrel's mum would bring the baby in to me at feeding time. I felt angry that she was so confident with Stephen and even had him in her room at night. It seemed she was taking over my baby.

I had never known what it was like to be seriously ill. I had barely had a sick day in my life. I also didn't recognise the symptoms. I couldn't sit on a chair, I had to kneel at the table to eat. I should have been hospitalised, but I had been traumatised from the only time I had ever spent in a hospital. I was afraid to go back. The infection worsened and the left cheek of my face started to swell, causing so much pain that I spent much of the day bathing it with hot salt water to relieve the agony. Darrel's mother rang work and got her leave extended.

An unfamiliar sound woke us up one morning after we had managed to catch a couple of hours' sleep. It didn't sound like anything I had heard before, and then I realised it was coming from Gran's room. I hobbled to her room with Darrel behind me. She was sitting up in bed making strange noises and grabbing at the air in front of her. I tried to talk to her but she was unaware that we were in the room.

'I think she's had a stroke,' Darrel said to me.

He called the ambulance and my Uncle Fred. There wasn't much left to do except wait for them to turn up. So Darrel left for work. Uncle Fred arrived. Walking into the kitchen unannounced, his piercing blue eyes bored into me. There was no smile on his mouth. Twenty seconds of complete silence, then out poured his fury.

'Look at her! Look at the state she's in. You were supposed to look after her!'

I shrugged. *Was I? I didn't know that.*

An Awkward Fit

He was so intent on yelling at me that he failed to notice that I was on my knees using the table to hold myself up. (I still couldn't sit after being home from hospital for four weeks).The pain in my face was agonising and only the hot salt water seemed to temporarily ease the throbbing. I was 19 and my world was in chaos. I was in almost total stupor. I was speechless. No one would have heard me, anyway, because by this time Stephen was screaming his lungs out.

'He is the nastiest man I have ever come across,' was the only comment Darrel's mother made.

Gran never came back. She moved to a nursing home a short distance away.

Looking in the mirror, I didn't recognise the bizarre features that looked back at me. After two days of bathing with the salt water, the left side of my face had blown up like a vivid red balloon. My left eye and part of my nose were no longer detectable. Darrel was beside himself with worry.

'That's it.' He bundled Stephen and me into the car. 'We're going to the bloody hospital. I'm going to find out what the hell's going on.'

An hour later, I was back in the Queen Victoria hospital surrounded by six doctors, all trying to find the source of my infection. I was mystified. They were confused. Next thing I remember was being put into a taxi and sent to the dental hospital. They forgot to tell me their diagnosis. It was only when I arrived at my destination that I knew what was happening. Stephen was still at the maternity hospital. The infection had wreaked havoc through my body and surfaced in my gums in the form of an abscess. The dentist stuck a cup under my top teeth; my pain was so intense that I didn't feel the blade slicing my gum, filling the cup with the contents of the abscess.

It was unbelievable. The pain disappeared instantly. I was given a prescription for antibiotics, put in a taxi for the twenty-five minute journey home and, by the time I arrived, the swelling had almost disappeared. I had a nose again and, although a bit the worse for wear, I was able to smile. I had entered the world of the living.

'Hi,' I beamed at Darrel, who was sitting in the kitchen alongside his mother looking like they had the weight of the world on their shoulders. I bounded through the door. The relief I felt was so great, I was laughing deliriously. The look on their faces was that of disbelief. We immediately drove to the maternity hospital to collect Stephen. As the antibiotics took effect, I started feeling well again and was able to cope a lot better. As my health improved, so did Stephen.

'I feel like he's my baby,' she said. It was time for Darrel's mother to go home. She had helped us out for about six weeks. Honestly, we would never have managed without her, but instead of being grateful, I was jealous of her. I felt as though she had taken over my life, including my baby, and I did not feel very grateful at that time. I was very young and resented her for so capably doing what I was not able to. My mother-in-law had formed a close bond with Stephen and had become quite possessive of him. I have to say that the day we took her to the Franklin Street bus depot and put her on the bus I was happy to see her go and have my family back. It was so difficult for her to leave and she cried all the way back home to Loxton. This bond she shared with our son grew stronger and stronger over the years.

By now he was three months old and the constant crying eased. But to us it seemed to go on for years. We had survived, and as Stephen grew so did my stomach with a new child. On 18 April 1970, 12 months and four days after Stephen was born, I gave birth to our daughter Nicole.

CHAPTER 2 - 1970s – The Chook House

I look down at my trophies and my old school books. Once again I reach into the worn and tattered cardboard box. I hesitate as my mind is triggered to search. My surroundings dissipate as I turn my attention upwards, diving deep into memory; can I find it and let the past become the present? The present slips away, I search further for feelings and thoughts. The memory is complete; WOW, how I've changed. I've become acutely aware I'm the only one who will ever know, the only one who can keep a record of my life, of past events.

How can I mourn the past for what it is – 'the past'?

Knowing all will be lost and forgotten in time brings sadness and yearning pain! Like a leaf in the wind I shiver and my heart cries out. In self-preservation I'm jolted back to the present before sadness overwhelms me and depression sets in (what a buzz). With the words 'life is cruel' ringing true in my mind; I now place an item without heed into the new box, neatly with love.

To be given life and the universe is to know the beauty of love. Then to watch it all fade into the past knowing one day it all will be taken away. It made me realise how precious and significant the present is. How wonderful and amazing it all is. That all those living today share this amazing thing. These things should make everyone feel an incredible passion toward each other because we don't have life for very long!

The existence of life is so special while death makes it so much more precious. Why can't people keep this in their conscious thoughts always? So they might celebrate life in harmony, or at least try a little harder. Is it any wonder that I shut myself away from the world? 1974. I remember the way in which our house was back in Salisbury. I remember that it was house number 38. The sitting room at that time looked fairly big for me at my age.

As you walked in the front door, straight opposite you there was the door to the kitchen in the opposite wall. To the left was the door to my parents' room. If you looked to the right you could see the fireplace that was blocked over with a heater in front. We used to have a kero heater before the electric one was bought. Walking through the kitchen door, my room was to the left, and next door was my sister Nicole's room. In my room there was a large clown face painted by Mum. The bed lined the other wall and the door could be seen in front of you if you sat at the head. To the right were the window and a large set of drawers with a wardrobe in the furthest corner.

We had two rabbits, both were white; they had babies (they all died). Then Penny, our dog, dug her way in underneath and tore through the netting and was chasing them around inside the cage. They both lived but one day got out of the cage and disappeared.

I remember when I was two or three years old, riding on one of the box-shaped plastic motorcycles with four black plastic wheels; mine had a red body and handlebars. The two front wheels were close together, so whenever you pushed it over one of the cracks in the split-level concrete you simply went arse up.

One of my first recollections was of my constant fascinations with the primary school across the road. I would stand and watch the children from inside the front screen door of our house.

I remember standing at the door looking through the screen at the kids playing during recess and lunch. I couldn't wait to get there like all the big kids. I was not quite old enough for school. My sister Nicole and I went to a nursery school that was run by Catholic nuns, while my mum went to work. I remember quite clearly my first day. It's quite an experience at the age of three years to be led down a corridor and enter a room where you turn around to see your mother disappearing through the door with a tear in her eye, with the all-too-clear knowledge that the door handle provides the only escape from what seems to be your new home. To be reunited with your mother is beyond your reach. Well, as with most children, new places, people and toys soon occupy your attention. But one difference in my case was that I never quite fitted in. I found that adapting to such a different environment, society and attention from which I had received at home was something I had difficulty with. Nicole still thinks it was Kym and me who locked her in the smashed-up cars at the back of the nursery. I wasn't even there, it was Anthony and Kym. I remember because Nicole was telling Mum when we got home, but I've never bothered correcting her.

Very early I developed a zest for life, a grand opinion of how good it was to be alive. I was only about four years old when I thought that even though there were some rough times, all in all it was pretty good to watch and see all the things around me. Lots of things I didn't see the importance of. There was so much to see that I hadn't seen or done before.

I learnt to cherish every moment, good and bad, and see the value of all that comes about. I saw that everything that occurred around me was incredible, in that no other would see and experience it exactly the way I would. I lived in Salisbury for nine years, and things that would seem to most to be of minor significance, to me had influence on my personality and character.

Well, the day finally came when I was old enough to go to school. I was so excited my first day, but as with a lot of occasions it turned out to be a disaster. It was a very wet, cold day and I was climbing on the play equipment when the boy ahead of me stepped back right into my eye and I fell off the equipment into a pile of mud. I went home with clothes on from the lost property box, my wet muddy things in a bag, and an explanation note from my teacher.

The next couple of years at school were quite good; although I felt uncomfortable with a lot of children, I did have a couple of friends. I liked most of the other children but I felt separated or distanced from them, and found it very difficult to communicate with them. At recess and lunch times I would sit on a bench in the playground and play my small guitar that my parents had given me one Christmas. I remember going to get the lunches from the canteen, punching all the bags holding pies and pasties of the boys and girls that I didn't like, who were horrible to me.

I enjoyed playing sports, and with the encouragement of my parents I joined the cricket and soccer teams. I wasn't one of their best players but my parents would support me and come along to watch me play. I have no idea why but even then I didn't feel like I was part of the team I felt I desperately wanted to be. I knew that I was no different to the others but I still felt strange. I had a really good friend Kym who also joined the sports teams.

There was also Wayne who lived two houses up from me. He and I used to light fires in the pipes in the preschool playground using caps and tissue or newspaper until Dad caught us trying to light a fire in a pine tree with matches. He was furious, he thought it was my friend's idea, and I would never have tried such a thing if I hadn't been talked into it, but I was just as much to blame as he was. We spent a lot of weekends and holidays at my grandparents' who lived in Loxton. I recall sitting in Nana's mulberry

tree, which over looked the chook house, stuffing myself
with mulberries. We used an old cooking pot with no
handle to collect them in. My cousins, Nicole and I used to
all play in the mandarin tree at the back (not one of us
could fit in it now).

Have you ever played the game of 'Lock Your Nana in the
Chook House?' I have.
It's true; I must admit it – I remember a bit vaguely
locking Nana in for almost three hours.
The chook house, which is only three to four feet high,
seems a great place to capture your grandmother at the
age of six. But you ought to be glad you weren't there
when I let her out. She was not the loving Nana I was used
to – she was fuming!

The worst part was that there was also a duck in with the
chooks. Nanna had just washed and set her hair and the
duck had shit all over her. Nana says it was three hours
but I doubt if it was that long. I remember thinking it was
funny. I think I must have gone and played for a while
and forgotten she was in there.
Penny, being a cocker spaniel, liked to hunt, and
unfortunately the only animals suitable to hunt were the
chickens next door. She decided to dig her way under the
fence into their chook house and had great fun running
around and biting the necks of about eight chooks and
leaving them half-dead and bleeding. The neighbour was
furious, and unfortunately it was Dad's birthday, so when
he arrived home from work Mum said, 'Happy birthday,
and darling. Guess what? Your dog has half-killed most of
the neighbour's chooks.'Ouch! Poor Dad had to go next
door and put the chooks out of their misery and then pay
our neighbour the price of some new ones. Dad was so
mad that he brought home one of the dead chooks and
tied it around Penny's neck and left it there for a week. I
think he thought it would stop the dog from attacking the

chooks again, but instead it was us who suffered. The smell was so bad that we couldn't go out and play in the backyard. Each day Mum got angrier and angrier with Dad, but he refused to untie the dead chook until the week was up. It didn't do anything for the dog at all. Dad was so naive; someone that he worked with told him this would work.

I'd like to tell you of the adventure taken to catch my first fish. It was rather an exciting day, for Dad was trying out a new motorised boat. While Mum and I sat patiently, Dad cast us off then jumped in and started our way down river. About half an hour later we decided to go around the bend and see if we would have better luck there, for up to now we had caught nothing. By this time Mum started to get sick and tired of fishing, plus the fact that it was getting very cold very quickly, so Dad turned the boat around, and to my utmost surprise, my fishing line began to tug violently.

Almost immediately, Dad rushed to my end of the boat and started helping me wind in my fish. When eventually the line with the fish on the end was in the boat and the excitement had calmed down, Dad started the boat for home. In the meantime, a storm of fairly strong wind and force was brewing up about half a mile up river. When Dad saw the storm, he looked a little worried but said we'd beat it. But that wasn't quite true, as we rounded the bend in the river we hit the storm head on and the water became pretty rough and tossed the boat around. Mum began to panic, the boat lurched side-ways and she over-balanced and next thing I was yelling and became quite upset. My parents thought I was scared but I was upset because Mum was sitting on my fish.

~

An Awkward Fit

Stephen and Nicole were ready.

'Let's go, kids! Time to go.' I walked them across the road to the school.

By the time we had reached the gate, Stephen was walking sideways, one eye on me and one on the gate and a broad grin across his face. He knew what was coming next. As soon as I made the move, he took off at great speed across the school grounds with me hot on his heels. I only ever caught up with him once. I knew he didn't want the other kids to see him kiss his mum goodbye, so I made sure I didn't catch up to him; but it was fun. I couldn't play the game with Nicky because she was only too happy to give me a hug in the schoolyard. We had an agreement that he would always love me and cuddle me until the day I died as long as it wasn't in front of his school-mates.

I was supposed to grow old loving both my children, he was not supposed to die before me. He promised he would love me until the day I died. He broke that promise. Why do I feel such anger?

What a reality shock it must have been for Stephen when he started going to school. What is so sad about the whole deal is that from the moment he learnt to crawl and could see the children across the road at the school, he desperately wanted to be old enough to be with them.

He started school in the mid-year intake. It was the middle of winter and a very cold wet day, but nothing could deter him from what he had been looking forward to for as long as he could remember. The simple act of walking across the road each day to finally be where he had dreamed of propelled him into a world of mystery and confusion, although we had no idea this was happening. This should have been a simple transition, a pleasant experience; not the beginning of what would become a nightmare for him.

It was mid morning, a day like any other. Routine. I opened the screen door and stepped out onto the veranda, still badly in need of the polish I promised it. I then walked out onto the spongy kikuyu lawn. Number 38 International Avenue was just another housing trust maisonette like the 28.hundreds of others in working class Salisbury North. To relieve the drabness and sameness I had planted several rose bushes along the front fence. From where I stood I looked directly across International Avenue into Salisbury North West Primary School's playground … and the small boy sitting alone.

I had noticed Stephen often sat by himself at recess time. He played his toy guitar, leaning against a brick wall at the end of the row of classrooms, which extended into a large asphalt area. He looked so alone – even the courtyard he sat in looked vast and empty, though other children were playing in small groups.
Why? Why isn't he playing with the other children? What's wrong with him?
He's normal. He's friendly and intelligent. Why is he so often alone?

The sight of Stephen sitting by himself in that playground distressed me – my heart went out to him. I was overcome with the urge to rush to him, rescue him, and comfort him. But I was powerless. Inadequate. Eventually I arranged to meet his grade 3 teacher. Miss Rogers was an attractive auburn-haired woman in her early twenties. She sat patiently listening to my concerns about Stephen and how upsetting it was to constantly watch him sitting alone and how frequently he came home telling me he didn't have a good day. How he had been picked on or he had had a fight with some boy in his class.
'He is unique, a very creative boy, and a self-motivated individual. He is very determined – once he has his mind set, he keeps insisting on going ahead with his ideas to the end.'

An Awkward Fit

She went on. 'Unfortunately, he finds it very hard to work with others and sometimes this leads to conflict. He is a very truthful person. I have found this personality trait to come out especially when I ask him about his behaviour. His only major weakness seems to be his concentration (his memory span), which is very short at times.'

It also became apparent during the conversation with Miss Rogers that Stephen had other abilities: he loved writing stories, building and constructing things.

One time it was a train with about four carriages so big that he needed help to carry it home; another time it was an airplane made out of cardboard and it was bigger than he was. In fact, once he started on a project, it was very hard for him to stop and try to turn his attention elsewhere. His teachers thought it was a good thing to encourage this skill. Often I would go to the school looking for Stephen and find he was the only one left in the classroom with the teacher, writing stories or building something. Not wanting to interrupt his concentration, she would stay until he completed his project. Stephen rarely did anything 'inside the square.'

These projects continued throughout his life. I dreamed of great things for him. He was smart; he had good spoken language skills at an early age, and he was full of confidence and determination.

Although I have tried countless times to pinpoint the first occasion I became conscious that there was something special or different about Stephen, I have never been able to be certain of the time or the place. As a small child, he was happy and well adjusted to his environment.

Although I was often anxious, his complexity confused me. It worried me that he didn't seem to be able to get along with other children very well. I recognised that, although he was intelligent, and absorbed knowledge quickly, he didn't have the social competencies that were appropriate for his age group. He could talk as well as any child about a subject that interested him, although he tended to give an over-detailed account.

Each time my concerns surfaced, I managed to convince myself I was worrying needlessly. *My kid's going to be all right.* He had a sharp mind and was very creative. There was so much potential that his future looked very bright and he could be anything he wanted to be. I loved the way he always wanted to help me fix things, although it drove Darrel crazy the way Stephen always wanted to take over.

It was mid morning. Another routine day. Darrel had caught the train to work,
Stephen and Nicky had gone to school, and I was in my dressing-gown at the kitchen table nursing my second cup of coffee. My kid's going to be all right. However, despite my youth and inexperience as a mother, my instincts told me something was different. He didn't quite fit in. At that stage in my life, I was more of a big sister to my children than a mother. I was enjoying life, and doing fun things with my children. I didn't want to become involved with trying to delve deeper into why life wasn't being too kind to my young son. I sealed off that part of my mind that was suggesting that he was special and different.
The teaching staff at his school and the organisations to which he belonged never picked up any major concerns. His reports generally said that his grades were quite good and he worked well in class, though he seemed segregated from his classmates and should try more to get on with them. The worst that could be said of him was that, at times, he could be infuriatingly vague.
Try more to get on with them.
How crazy was that? How was he going to pick up such a skill?

An Awkward Fit

I believed that social interaction was a skill that most of us are born with, and Stephen simply didn't seem to have that skill. Children liked him but got sick of him wanting to explain how to do something because he could see the broader picture, he could always see a different and often better way of doing things. He had to work very hard at even understanding the reasons others did what they did. None of us understood the pressure we were placing on him with our expectations.

I remember watching him play junior district soccer on Saturday afternoons. He didn't appear any different from the other children. In fact, he was just as good, just as clever and just as attractive – even better looking than some of the other players. Yet watching Stephen as goalkeeper during those Saturday matches I couldn't shake off my unease and disquiet. *Why? Is it a mother's intuition? Am I imagining his difference? He's just like any other kid his age. But there's something, what is it?*
I was like any other parent who has a desire for his or her child to fit in. I don't think anyone knew what was going on with Stephen or even what I was feeling about him. I couldn't understand it myself. I thought maybe I was just being over-protective.

I recall Nicky telling how she always felt protective of her brother Stephen. She said he came over as somewhat aloof and a loner.
'I have to stick up for him, Mum. He's like an absent minded professor and he doesn't have many friends.'
Nicky's up front support was lost on Stephen; he frequently came home from school protesting he didn't need his sister to fight his battles.
'Sometimes it's embarrassing,' he said.

Life for us as a family unit went on. Stephen was now eight years old and Nicky was seven. I had recently celebrated my 28th birthday and Darrel, at 30, was pursuing his career with

Telecom as a linesman, and made extra cash pumping petrol at the local service station. I also worked part-time at the same service station. Everything seemed normal. Life was good. During those years I didn't share my concerns over Stephen with my husband. Darrel's life was uncomplicated and straightforward; he was supportive of his wife and children and was a good breadwinner. It was, however, in the summer of 1978 the first real serious incident involving Stephen occurred.

In the 1950s and '60s, my father, Arthur, had been heavily involved with the scout movement as a scoutmaster. Much later Darrel himself had been a senior scout with the local group in Loxton. Maybe it was only natural to encourage Stephen to become a scout. But I had an ulterior motive. I felt Stephen, as part of a group mixing with children who had common interests and a policy of acceptance, would increase his ability to understand and get along. I was wrong.

It was early evening, shortly after dropping him off at only his first or second meeting as a newly invested scout; there was a knock on our door. Darrel and I were watching television in the lounge room. I turned the sound down and switched on the porch light, opening the door. There on the front porch was one of the scout leaders looking very apologetic, with Stephen in tow.

'Sorry. I'm not sure how this happened,' said the scout leader, nudging Stephen forward. My son was covered in bright red and green dye and his blonde hair was streaked with green. As he looked up at me a blob of green liquid dropped smoothly down from his fringe and ended up on the tip of his nose. I reached out and wiped it off. At the same time my eyes explored his face for signs of stress but there were none.

Somehow, he'd managed to tie-dye himself. My mind raced with the possibilities that had resulted in Stephen being covered in the horrible mess – had he wanted to do things his way again, and angered the others who had then up-ended the dye over Stephen's head? Or was this the result of one of his many accidents?

On a later date Stephen came home, sore with bruises over much of his face. He was angry, telling how he was thrown through a closed door by other scouts while the leaders were out of the room. Stephen hung in with the scout movement. Determination and persistence were two of his admirable traits, but again I was hit with the nagging thoughts: *How did this happen? Why does everything happen to him?* I took some consolation that most of Stephen's injuries were not serious. Since his eighth birthday, Stephen had become increasingly involved in 'incidents' and 'injuries.'

There were no bones broken and I never had to rush him to casualty for stitches. I didn't realise that although there was no physical damage being done to this small boy's body, a whole lot of damage was happening in his young mind. How did I react to these frequent mishaps? I took them in my stride and patched him up each time with a bandaid. My theory was if I made no fuss it wouldn't make him feel clumsy or useless. Sometimes the childhood incidents were more than just clumsy mishaps – a near fatal fire in the pine tree where Stephen was playing with a friend was one such episode.

CHAPTER 3 – 1978 - New school, new beginning

In grade 4, I made friends with Mark who lived in the street behind us. I remember playing on one of the big cable reels over at the school between the fence and a tree. A branch from the tree stretched out over the reel and fence. It was thin and very spindly.

One day I asked Mark to hold the branch down by hanging on the end while I climbed onto it. I let go of the branch and leant over to climb on, when all at once I saw stars and found myself on the ground looking up at the reel where I was standing a moment before.
My lip and cheek were bleeding something chronic. Mark had let go of the branch and I copped it full in the face.

Another injury that I would have to tell Mum about.

I feel sad when I remember my Uncle Wayne, my memory of him is so clear. He is my mother's brother, my favourite uncle. I remember watching him play on the lawn under the clothesline with the family dog Jerry, an overweight part – dachshund part – terrier with little stumpy legs and a long body. This was at Loxton on my mother's parents' fruit orchard. I remember him coming home from work and taking me on his bike to his girlfriend's.

My mum had a similar relationship with her brother Wayne, as do I with my sister. A week before Wayne died on the Saturday morning my dad came into the dining room where we were eating breakfast; he said that he had had a strange dream. He turned to Uncle Wayne and said, 'What flowers do you want on your coffin? I dreamt that you were killed on your motorbike. You need to be careful.' A week later Uncle Wayne was killed in a motorbike accident, he was 18 and I was six years old.

Once when we went to get Nicole from gymnastics I played in the playground on one of those merry-go-round things. On this occasion when I didn't want to leave the playground Mum threatened to go without me if I didn't get in the car. On one particular occasion I didn't even get a chance to get in the car. Mum must have been preoccupied because she drove off without me.

About 20 minutes later when I was getting rather upset Mum drove up laughing and at the same time very upset. She was so intent on driving home, she forgot about me. I remember when Mum was playing the trumpet in the Salvation Army band and practising at home. That's when we went to Sunday school and scoffed on the paper shell almonds out the back of the Army hall.

Another time my grandfather was having a row with my nanna, and the pet budgie Bluey was sitting in his cage listening to what was going on. My grandfather, who was pretty upset by the whole affair, kept on walking around saying that no one loved him, that no one loved him except Bluey. But when my grandfather approached the cage and said, 'You love me, Bluey, don't you?' the budgie replied, 'Aah! Shut up, Morrie.'

~

January 1979, we moved to Craigmore, a new northern suburb housing estate only 16 kilometres from our old International Avenue address. It was a hot summer's day and we had spent an exhausting week cleaning the old house, stripping off wallpaper and removing junk that had been collecting over the ten years living at Salisbury North.

The Craigmore house was new. It was a corner house at the bottom of the court. Darrel had chosen a white-bricked house. 'It'll be much cooler in summer,' he said. What I liked about the house was its unexpected spaces and its hidden closets.

A new school for Stephen meant a head full of interest and excitement. With a new school came the promise of a new start. It also meant new teachers and new friends and classmates for both children.

Stephen wanted to learn guitar. I felt pleased and Darrel was proud. As a young boy, Darrel had learnt the guitar and clarinet and he felt that his son was following in his footsteps. From the age of four, Nicole had been in gymnastics so we were anxious to cultivate something in Stephen also. We bought him a three-quarter sized guitar for Christmas and enrolled him in private lessons through an advertisement in the local paper. This particular music teacher taught classical guitar, and that is how Stephen was introduced to this style of playing. Stephen immersed himself in practice for many hours, and became quite good.

For Christmas that year, his nana gave him the most disgusting teddy bear I had ever seen. She had knitted it. It looked like a vagrant. The teddy was about 12 inches long and was a mushroom colour. It had two old trouser buttons for eyes and was stuffed with old stockings, which seeped through the holes that appeared in the knitting. It was gruesome.

When Stephen opened his present I could see the disbelief and disappointment. The look on his face said it all. He was too old for such a teddy, definitely one that looked raggedy and homemade. To my surprise, that teddy got a lot of use over the next five years, and I still have it today. Whenever Stephen was hurting or upset over something, he'd go into his room and cuddle that unsightly old teddy and regularly fell asleep with it beside him.

We were often frustrated and angry with Stephen over some of the crazy and unusual ways he did things, giving him our usual lectures or demanding an explanation. He would start grinning. I could see he was trying desperately not to smile and look serious, but he couldn't. I invariably ended up smiling myself, because he looked so funny trying not to laugh about a serious situation. I remember thinking I didn't want to spoil his sense of humour, and that I couldn't possibly tell him off for grinning.

Stephen's teacher for both grade 6 and 7 was David Saywell, a six-foot league football player and an extremely competent teacher whose students were in awe of him. Another talent the teacher possessed was playing the guitar and he taught his students several popular songs. Stephen would take his guitar to school and accompany him and later come home with his head filled with songs from 'The Little River Band'.

We spent many relaxing hours at home listening to the gentle sounds of classical music as Stephen practised. Stephen had a real gift with the guitar. We were so proud that I guess we went a bit over the top and when friends visited we boasted about how beautifully he played and would often get Stephen to play for them. What we didn't realise, and only found out when my sister Jan mentioned to me, was that Nicole felt left out. We appeared to her to be more interested in Stephen than in her. What a very easy, thoughtless mistake for us to make. We certainly hadn't meant her to feel this way, but sometimes when one child needs a lot of guidance and support, this can happen.

Grade 7 was a good year for Stephen. He finished with an average of 81.2 per cent. The interesting comment his teacher made was that, at times, Stephen could be 'infuriatingly vague'. Stephen had many good qualities about him. It was easy to be positive about his future. There was always something new he wanted to try. He wanted to be someone important. Most of all, he wanted to be rich.

Stephen came up with the idea of maybe going to a secondary school where he could continue his music. We had heard the Fremont High School had a music centre, which was set up to cater for students with a gift for music. The school was five kilometres from home and one of only four schools in the state with a special music suite for talented students. Darrel and I were very nervous when Stephen was required to audition and attend an interview. This was an opportunity that didn't come along every day.

In 1982 he was accepted into the school to study classical guitar and clarinet. Since moving to Craigmore I had become more settled in my mind about Stephen. He seemed to have adjusted better to his new environment.

The following year Nicky went to the same high school. She took up playing the flute. It was not long before Stephen's complexities surfaced again. He was having difficulty understanding and coping with his peers. He spoke of other students and how he found it hard to cope with their tactless banter and frivolity.

After I contacted Stephen's teacher Elizabeth Harlock-Lea whilst writing this book, she wrote to me, giving her impressions of her student:

Stephen was a highly talented classical guitarist and became very competent on the clarinet as second study instrument. He participated with enthusiasm in the classical guitar ensemble and various concert bands at the school.

Stephen did have a unique personality. I remember him smiling and enjoying a joke; I also remember him being withdrawn and vague at times. However, given his talent in music and mathematics, we did tend to assume that Stephen's behaviour was somewhat like an 'absentminded professor'.

At times, one could sense his frustration and unease. At other times Stephen was quite laid back. Stephen's circle of school friends was limited. In my perception because he was shy, but also discriminating about his choice of friends. Stephen was a caring young man. He was sensitive in his own right and to the needs of others. He had clearly had a difficult struggle. The differences in him that we did not clearly understand when he was at school fell into place ...

In 1982-83 neither Darrel nor I were aware of Stephen entering or achieving credits in both state maths competitions until the father of another student happened to say how terrific it was that both our sons had done so well. Stephen had a couple of really good friends and often spent weekends staying with them.

Axel was 14 when he joined Stephen's year nine class at high school. Axel's family had migrated from Germany. The parents spoke very little English, but Axel and his sister, who was a year older than he, spoke it fluently.

Axel and Stephen hit it off from the start and became good friends. Both were determined young lads with fixed ideas and a lot of living to do. Axel also had visions of greatness. It was an interesting relationship. They were similar in many ways and often became frustrated with each other, but they remained friends. Axel often came on outings with us and they spent many weekends at each other's homes, which meant we also became friendly with Axel's parents.

One weekend, Axel was staying with us. The two boys went off bike riding for the day. They hadn't returned home by late afternoon. I started to get anxious. Finally, they turned up at dusk – Axel was fuming. They hadn't been able to agree which route to take but Stephen had won and they went in the direction that he had chosen. However, he wouldn't turn back when it came time to head home. They ended up riding for hours. Axel was not at all impressed. In fact, when they arrived home he was so angry he could hardly speak.

Another weekend we took Axel with us to our friend's farm in the north. The men were out feeding the sheep from the ute. Darrel was in front with Geoff, who was driving slowly, and the boys were in the back with the feed. Their job was to cut the string on the bales and drop them over the side. Axel cut the string on the bale Stephen was sitting on and he tumbled face-first off the back, scraping the skin off his face as he hit the ground. Such mishaps often happened to Stephen. It wasn't that he lacked coordination, but it was more a case of him being in the wrong place at the wrong time, or misjudging the situation.

Another time, when he rode his bike to the shop he came home with his face and elbow bleeding. He hadn't looked where he was going; his mind was elsewhere and he rode into a parked car. Each year during the Christmas school holidays Stephen, Nicky and I worked in the apricot harvest. Our friends Kevin, Meg and Greg owned a fruit orchard at Taylorville, across the river north of Waikerie in South Australia's Riverland. And they were happy to have us camp on their property on the bank of the River Murray for the duration of our working holiday.

When I was young, my father had also owned an orchard at Taylorville, before moving to Waikerie and later to Loxton. Our children were young and active and I was keen to have them experience the enjoyment of the lifestyle I had grown up with. At the same time, though, I wanted them to appreciate the need to work to earn money. Working in the education system meant I had a six-week break over Christmas to enjoy this time with them.

We pitched our large tent in a beautiful area next to the creek that flowed into the property through an inlet from the river. Kevin had made this area into a park for friends and workers; it had a toilet and shower block and power outlets. Several other families working in the harvest also camped in the park.

An Awkward Fit

Each morning at eight o'clock we walked the short distance to the shed where we spent the day cutting apricots and placing them on trays to be dried. Darrel was not on holidays, but he would come and stay with us on weekends.

I often sat on a large tree trunk that had fallen some time ago, and stretched quite a way into the creek. Only parts of it were visible above the water, and if I wasn't careful climbing out on it I'd have ended up in the creek. This log was a little further up the creek from where the children swam. It was my favourite place to be alone.

Once I sat there for a very long time, staring out into the creek and admiring the beautiful red gums that lined the banks. It would be impossible to count the number of times we'd swum and skylarked in that spot over the years. Small incidents and visions of those times have drifted into my mind as I've been writing this.

In my daydream I can see Nicky, about nine years old, in her blue bathers with the pink stripe. Her light brown hair, just past her shoulders, is wet and straight. She is swimming with Stephen, who is a year older. I don't remember his bathers but I can see his long slender build, his long legs. He is tanned, with hair bleached- blond from hours in the sun. They are diving to the bottom of the creek to collect handfuls of clay, which they dump on the bank and later mould into little round pots they give to Kevin.

One weekend when Darrel was visiting, we had been cutting apricots. It had been an intensely hot and tiring day working in the apricot cutting shed, so after work we headed to the creek for a swim. Darrel volunteered to stay behind and cook our evening meal, which he did in the electric frying pan. He called us when it was ready and the kids had a race to see who could get back first. At the same moment that the children reached the opening of the tent, Darrel emerged with the hot frying pan, looking for somewhere to put it to cool down. He was wearing only shorts, and came through the tent opening as Stephen approached at full pelt. Seeing that a collision was inevitable Stephen made a split-second decision. He put his hands out, an action that pushed the frying pan into his father's stomach. Darrel screamed. The pan burnt him severely and all that night he groaned as I frequently put ice on his burns. He should have gone to hospital, it was so bad. Poor Stephen was not a popular son for quite a while, and Darrel wore a distinct shape of that frying pan on his stomach for many weeks.

Isolated incidents, Stephen's mishaps and accidents may have seemed to be part of a normal teenager's growing up. However, viewed collectively over a period of time, a pattern seemed to be emerging. I asked myself: *Was this clumsiness? Did he have a misfire in his brain? Was he accident-prone?* Stephen certainly had a thought pattern different from the rest of us. It took some time, but I was to find out later, risk taking and recklessness was a likely indicator of things to come: 'Schizophrenia.'

CHAPTER 4 -1986 - Wackery at Waikerie

My parents exist as a source of stress, highlighting a depressing reality concerning the future results of failing to devote myself to studying. Having to be reminded of this many times proves uncomfortable and annoying.

Anyone would resent this source of discomfort, which to my misfortune is schoolwork. And, as a result, I automatically try to avoid contact with them. The finding is merely that my parents must stop reminding me of my homework. How would he (Dad) like it if each night when he came home from work I reminded him of all the jobs he had to do around the house? Mr Twigden [Kevin] can't handle individuality and chaos, diverse characters and personalities. I feel his frustration with me.

~

Why did Stephen write this in his journal? Could it be because of some of the situations he found himself in? I remember one incident at harvest time in the Riverland when Kevin had given Stephen a job loading pumpkins into a large wooden bin attached to the back of the tractor. Darrel and I were with Kevin driving past the pumpkin patch. I looked out the window and there was our son hard at work, except he was sitting on the top of the tractor over the engine with his back towards the direction the tractor was headed. He had his head turned looking over his shoulder and his hands on the steering wheel. He was driving the tractor back to front. I froze. *My God! What was he doing?*

The load of pumpkins in the trailer had become too heavy and the front wheels of the tractor were raised off the ground. Stephen had worked out that if he put his weight on the front of the tractor it would be enough to keep the front wheels on the ground while he drove.

This was out of the square. It was not the normal way people would solve this problem. Instead of taking some of the pumpkins out of the bin, he chose to do it his way. I think it was ingenious! I probably would have thought similarly, but wouldn't have acted upon my thoughts because it was not an accepted way of doing things. *Please, please God, don't let Kevin see what he is doing.* Kevin didn't see and I breathed a sigh of relief.

This problem with the weight of the pumpkins was not a difficulty; it was a challenge, an opportunity to solve a problem. This was what life was like for Stephen. I guess this was most likely the sort of thing Stephen was referring to in his notes, when he said Kevin – 'Mr Twigden' – couldn't cope with individuality and chaos.

Stephen's enjoyment of working in the fruit harvest and the fact that my father had owned a property had their influence on him. He began asking Kevin questions about his property and showed an interest in fruit work. Given Stephen's love of the outdoors and interest in agriculture, Kevin pointed out the advantages of a future in this industry, using his eldest son as an example. Trevor had gone through Roseworthy Agricultural College and was an agricultural adviser. This sounded good to Stephen, who was highly motivated and ambitious about his future.

'It would be great, Dad. I could get a really good job with lots of money, or even buy my own fruit block.' These were the words coming from our very excited and enthused son when we sat down to talk to him about his future. He figured that after he'd completed his education he could land a well-paid job or, better still, be his own boss – and start at the top, no less. In his world, everything had to happen *now*, as if there was no tomorrow. There was no question of failure. He was going to be *somebody*. Why work on a fruit-block if you could own your own – or better still, become an agricultural adviser? It seemed that a future as a musician was no longer on the agenda. In a way, Stephen adopted his career ambitions from his friendship with Kevin and changed his focus from music to a rural pursuit. Kevin had made us a part of his extended family, and had a big influence on our children's careers. He certainly gave Stephen a positive direction.

As I've already mentioned, Stephen had difficulty coping with some of his peers at Fremont High School, and while we thought at the time that music could be his vocation, he became very interested in agriculture. I had no qualms about him changing direction. He was strong-willed, a quick learner and clever. I believed that, whatever he decided to do, he would stick with it and do well. I never doubted his ability to succeed. Following an agricultural career path might also have the benefit of allowing him the freedom he seemed to need to do things in his own unique way.

Stephen's grades at school were good, but probably not good enough to guarantee him a place at the agricultural college. He was in year ten and had two more years to complete his high school education. There was a way that he would stand a better chance of being accepted into college, and that was to do a two-year certificate course in agriculture at Urrbrae Agricultural High School. We discussed this option with him, and he was very enthusiastic about it. His interest in and knowledge of the land were beneficial in Stephen being accepted to do the course at Urrbrae. It meant abandoning his music studies. If he had any regrets about this move, we were not aware of them. I think Stephen was having difficulty coping with the added pressure of his music studies on top of his already busy schedule. A requirement of being a music student was that the students were to keep up with their normal school subjects as well as do well with their music studies. This meant Darrel and I were continually putting pressure on him to study.

Changing schools transformed Stephen's life. His first love was music. After a few weeks in his new school, he discovered a struggling but persistent music band made up of brass and string instruments. He became involved in transforming it. Life was good. His interest in the band and the practical work he was required to do with his studies played a vital role in Stephen's success.

Everything seemed to be fitting into place for him. To Darrel and I, it was relief – at last Stephen had found somewhere he fitted in. The other students appreciated him for his leadership skills and his obvious gift for music. He very quickly became one of the organisers, so that with his input and enthusiasm the band quickly grew in both size and proficiency, and band members started to become quite accomplished musicians.

Stephen enjoyed the agricultural studies and practical work. He even had a social life. He kept up his friendship with Axel, his school mate from the Fremont High school days, and a couple of others that he knew from his previous school.
'Mum, I've seen this really great black electric guitar. The guy said I could have it cheaper because it's the last one in the shop.' 'Get through this course and I'll buy you one,' I promised him. I felt his intense disappointment. Regretfully, I talked him out of it. I was afraid the guitar would become his main focus and would affect his studies, at the same time we really couldn't afford to buy it. But, not to be defeated, Stephen brought home one night the school's electric guitar and amplifier. He had borrowed them to practise at home.

The tuning on the amplifier didn't seem quite right to him so he decided to pull it apart bit by bit, piece by piece. I couldn't believe what I saw when I went into his room. The amplifier was spread in a million pieces over his bed and the floor. Every wire and screw was out, lying in neat little piles. I was horrified. I drew in a deep breath. *How's he going to fix this one?*

Next day it was all back together. 'Stephen, you will be in all sorts of trouble! They will never let you borrow anything again,' I said to him.

'Don't worry, Mum! They will never know the difference,' he reassured me – and, as usual, he was right.

It was a year and a half into Urrbrae and my previous anxieties over Stephen had subsided. I still thought I could read my son quite well. He and I were alike in many ways – we almost communicated without words. I could also read signs of stress and fear in his eyes and other body language when it was there. Some days sitting quietly watching Stephen tuning his guitar, I felt that familiar gut feeling: *Is he going to be all right? I'm still so scared for him. I'm still trying to convince myself he will be okay. But ....*

CHAPTER - 5 – 1987 - The cliffhanger

There's something badly missing in my life. What I need is a relationship that isn't just short-term or a one-night stand, but something that will last. I feel so alone and empty. A girlfriend seems to be the thing that I need most. I tend to push my family and friends away from me.

How can someone who's too emotionally withdrawn to show their real self expect someone to show an interest in them? I suppose that's why I get out and rage so much and do wild and crazy things, to make up for the gap, but it doesn't seem to work.

I am the sort of person who made it hard for others to find my true centre or personality because of the screen I placed around myself. When someone succeeds in penetrating that screen, I feel emotionally attached to them due to my suppressed desires to have a truly close girlfriend. Each time this occurs I find that the other isn't out for a lasting relationship but rather just a bit of temporary mutual fun and therefore I end up disappointed. When I finally find someone who feels the same way I do, I find it even harder to let myself go and become emotionally involved, no matter how much I try.

I have no illusion about what's reality and what isn't, although having to choose to adopt a realistic outlook on the world in general rather than screen out the reality and replace it with fantasy poses a psychological problem for me. I am tempted to fantasize about my life and the world in general because of the inbuilt fear of experiencing the depression that emotionally upsetting situations bring.
The sad part is there are heaps of people who feel the same way I do. It's a pity people can't be more understanding about those who are emotionally

withdrawn and becoming anti-social and give them a bit more help. You can never have too many friends.

I've just made an interesting discovery concerning action novels and have come to a conclusion that most science fiction has in some way a comment on or around Christian beliefs, which it contradicts, twists, or completely eradicates the existence of. Science fiction takes you away from all the pressures and struggles of reality. It also involves the way other people's minds work/function and nearly always works on honour and devotion towards people. This is the reason I indulge in reading these types of novels. Also, I feel comfortable with writing science fiction and intend to expand on this.

I believe authors play a game with the reader's curiosity. They know what's going to happen but they don't let on. Even if the reader has read it before he can still imagine the scenes or situation to be happening. For the first time I seem to want to give the whole scene away in my excitement and wanting to write my own stories. I get all excited when, after many days and weeks where my mind refuses to produce, it suddenly explodes with new ideas for essays. I just can't write fast enough when an idea comes to me, and therefore jump from one line of thought to the next before I can get it all down on paper.

~

It was during his final year at Urrbrae High School, while doing communication assignments, that Stephen discovered the world of science fiction and embraced it with a passion. Some assignments required the students to write responses, or sequels, to novels they had read. One of those novels Stephen chose was from David Eddings' Belgarian Series, and Stephen called his sequel 'Bound to Destinies.' His ability to portray and extend a novel in an exciting, mysterious way was affirmed by Bronte Price, his English teacher. Who wrote: Stephen, you have an exciting, rich style. Your use of vividly descriptive words builds up a clear picture in the reader's mind. To be quite frank, Stephen, books such as the Belgarian Series are not my normal reading fare. However, I thoroughly enjoyed reading your response to it. Why? I think especially because I was able to enter a completely different world while I read your work. Your writing not only enticed me to enter that world … it also maintained my presence there for the duration of the entire piece of work – not an easy task for a student writer. Stephen, would you please consider entering this as a short story in the Young Writers' Award?

One evening, at 17, Stephen brought Valerie home for dinner. She was a university student who lived in North Adelaide. Then there was Zoë, whom I never met, but I knew that he was very much smitten by her and when she broke up with him he was very hurt and confused. To him the mind of a female was very complex and he had difficulty understanding. 'I don't understand! She says she loves me but then she doesn't get in touch with me for days. I go around to the house and they tell me that she is going out with the father of the child she baby-sits. Someone is lying! I don't know who but I'm going to find out.' Stephen got caught up in an emotional whirlwind, 'I don't know if she still loves me. If she did, she would have got in contact with me by now. I feel like only one more thing can go wrong in my life before I break down and crack. With each day that passes, I can feel myself becoming more and more confused.'

Stephen's heart was breaking. It was his first real love and he really didn't know how to handle it. Back then, life for Darrel and me, during Stephen's teenage years, was full of surprises, uneasiness and apprehension. Each time we relaxed and felt he had settled down and things were working out for him, along came another obstacle.

For Nicole, it was frustration and wishing he could get his act together. She was excited about her brother going to Urrbrae. It was another chance for him to make friends and fit in. One day she confided in me, 'We're always spending our time fixing his problems. I feel life for me sometimes just isn't normal – I'm always caught up in the after-effects. It's a sort of mix of unease and confusion.'

Nicole's comments came as a shock. I always saw her as the perfect daughter – sensible grounded.

It's 1.00 am. I'm standing in the darkened hallway looking at Stephen's bedroom door. There is a light shining from underneath the door. There are sounds of scratching and clinking. It's 2.00 am. I'm standing in the darkened hallway looking at the light coming from beneath Stephen's door. There is a sound of scratching and shuffling.

It's 3.30 am. I'm standing in the darkened hallway again, staring at the light beneath Stephen's bedroom door. There are sounds now of Stephen's electric train moving along the track.

The bedside clock flashed 2.32 am and Darrel was shaking me out of a deep sleep.

'Helen, wake up! Helen.'

'What's wrong?' I whispered.

'Come out here and see if you can smell what I smell.' He left the bedroom, expecting me to follow. Half asleep, with my eyes still shut, I swung my legs onto the floor and at the same time felt for my dressing-gown at the end of the bed. Now fully awake, I crept through the front porch way, through the lounge room, carefully dodging the areas where the squeaky boards were, and entered the kitchen where Darrel was waiting for me. I sniffed the air. It was a strange, almost pleasant odour and was coming from the direction of our son's bedroom.

'Oh no, he's on marijuana!' I read Darrel's mind.

'Surely not – where would he get it?'

We looked in his room. It was empty. The screen was off the window and the winding mechanism had been removed, so that it was easy to step into and out of the window, like a doorway. We went back to the kitchen and sat in the dark, waiting. It was half an hour before we heard his bedroom window quietly being shut. We crept into the room and switched on the light, and there was Stephen just inside the window.

'What the hell are you up to...?' Darrel yelled.

Stephen chuckled and produced a handful of sparklers and small firecrackers. He grinned at us. 'I ran out, had to shoot over to Michael's place and get some more.'

I cannot leave out this next story. God must have been watching over him and decided it was not his time to leave us. There is no other explanation for him surviving this incident. On this particular weekend we were visiting Kevin and Meg Twigden at Taylorville. It was apricot harvest time. Stephen's friend, Kym, from his childhood days at Salisbury, was visiting his grandmother, about a half-hour drive away. Stephen asked if he could borrow our car to visit and stay overnight. He was still on his probationary driver's license. As my brother Wayne had died in a motorbike accident when he was 18, I held great fears for Stephen on the road and didn't want him to take the car. Darrel understood my feelings but said gently, 'We need to trust him. I'll take full responsibility.'

With a promise that he would be back by eight o'clock next morning, he drove off in our car. Eight o'clock came and went. There was no Stephen. My apprehension grew as the seconds ticked by, I tried not to worry. *He's only running late as usual.* At 9.30 am Kevin arrived at the park on his three-wheeler motorbike with some news. 'Stephen's not hurt but he had an accident on the way back here and there is some damage to the car.' With Kevin we headed towards Morgan.

We were worried about what we were going to find. My main concern was for Stephen; I knew he would be feeling devastated.

Just outside Morgan, we saw something that totally distracted us from our concerns. In the distance, on the road in front of us, we could see a great shower of sparks. It was an old Volkswagen with three young men, one driving and the other two hanging on to a rope that was tied on the driver's side and swung over the roof. The two men hanging on to the rope were balancing on the front passenger side of the car. The driver's side wheel was missing and they were trying to keep the axle from hitting the road as they drove along, without much success. This was causing the spray of sparks as the axle kept hitting the road. I have to say that I had never seen anything quite like this before.

It was fascinating, and Darrel and I burst out laughing. It certainly broke up the tenseness of our situation. We arrived at the accident scene to see our son standing at the top of the cliff, unhurt. Our car was not in sight. When we joined him, Stephen pointed to our Commodore at the bottom of an 18-foot cliff. The wheels were almost invisible, buried in drift sand .A large branch of a gum tree had passed through the driver's side window and out the rear window. It was a miracle the boy hadn't been killed, let alone being unhurt and only a little shaken. The tow truck operator said he had never seen anything like it in all his years of attending accidents.

Stephen had been heading back to our camp in good time, and he was driving down a dirt road that had been recently graded to remove dips. The holes had been filled in and covered with a layer of loose gravel resembling small marbles. It was almost impossible to walk on the surface without slipping, let alone drive on it at any reasonable speed. It was like a skating rink and, being an inexperienced driver, Stephen had lost control of the car as he turned the corner. He had spun around three times before lurching over the cliff.

CHAPTER – 6 – 1987 - Move to Roseworthy

I finished my exams on Monday and feel I did reasonably well. I've been fairly busy over the last few weeks trying to finish off my work and learn for my exams as well. I have written to Roseworthy Agricultural College hoping to be accepted to do a course in agriculture.

On Tuesday I must go to the police-recruiting department to submit an application form and have a physical check up in order to join the police force. This is just another door I'm keeping open in case I don't get into college. I'm signing my name in a first-aid course to help my chances of selection. I must put on another 4 kg to meet the weight requirements, so I've been eating heaps of fattening foods.

I am working part-time, at the moment at Hungry Jack's hamburger restaurant and soon starting full-time over Christmas, but I still have to convince Mum to let me stay in the house while they are at Waikerie for the apricot season. I am a little sad that school and my school friends will become a thing of the past, but I suppose I will become used to it.

~

Stephen was accepted into Roseworthy and moved onto campus to take up his studies towards a two-year Associate Diploma in Agricultural Production. He boarded during the week and came home on weekends. His room was in Block 2, a separate dormitory from the main buildings. The decision for Stephen to board at college was not made lightly.

Darrel and I discussed it with Stephen and together we agreed that it would be good for him – he would feel more independent, he would have access to the library and the computers and have a better relationship with the other students.

Stephen could scarcely hold his excitement in, he was so happy. This was what he dreamed of, this was success. Life was happening for him. Darrel and I went to help settle him in and saw the dormitory where he would be housed, for the first time. We were bitterly disappointed. We looked at the damaged wall panels and graffiti and wondered what sort of students had previously stayed there. Why had the college not repaired it before the new student intake?

Stephen's room was small but adequate for his needs, and the size didn't seem to worry him. He was excited about starting his college years and looking forward to the future, which, to all of us looked very promising.

Our concerns for Stephen began shortly after the start of the first semester. The first weekend he came home with a broken nose and lacerations to his left cheek under his eye. He said the injuries came from falling off a trampoline. I was upset, and a small voice inside me said, *Oh no, not again! Another injury. Why is he so careless?* But I didn't doubt his explanation as he said they'd been celebrating their arrival as new students on campus. We were concerned for him but said little, other than asking him to be more careful in the future. This was the first of several injuries Stephen sustained at college. Darrel and I felt concerned that there was more going on than what he was telling us; however, he was not prepared to elaborate. I let it go. After all, he was an adult.

Helen Maczkowiack

CHAPTER - 7 - 1987 - Life at College

This week at Roseworthy is known as Prank Week, where all the students play pranks on each other. Last night ten students shifted 200 bales of hay onto the front step of a farm staff office, blocking the door. The tractor was placed in the raceway to the dairy. Other tractors were placed out in paddocks.

Tonight some of the cows were painted green (it was a water-based paint) and a staff member's bike was put on top of a water tower. A full-size boat and a life-size statue of a horse were placed in the dining room. Because of the noise in the block that I'm in, I've decided to shift to a not-so noisy area. I'll probably move in on Friday. If I left my boots outside the door because I had been working with animals that day they would end up on the roof.

Last Monday I decided to go along to a Christian Fellowship meeting and surprised them by making most of the comments regarding the subject. I enjoyed it quite a lot and think I'll go next Monday as well.

Every Wednesday they have a film night on a big screen on the wall in the college club. Tonight they played the film The Last Emperor. It's a good movie but sad from beginning to end. Tomorrow I've got practical experience in the workshop, working with tractors and motors and other farm implements.

It's hard to study at times, because a lot of people in my class don't really have a positive attitude towards their work and want to party a lot. This is another reason why I want to shift rooms to a quiet area in a working type of atmosphere to give me more motivation. I still haven't quite gotten used to living away from home with no one to push me, but I'm trying to.

I was in my new room when Chris and friends were kicking my door, yelling abusive language and thumping at my window while I was trying to study at Roseworthy College.

Chris knocked on my door and pushed me off balance back into my room when I opened the door to tell them to go away. When I got up to stop Chris and friends from coming in, punches were thrown at me. I was then forced into the corridor where I tried to defend myself. I received blows to the left temple, eye and a number of other areas of the head. One of Chris's friends stopped the fighting and while trying to restrain me, invited others to join in.

Seeing that I could not possibly defend myself against all, I pulled free and left the corridor. I was told not to return. I know of no reason why I received such treatment. I can only assume it was because I didn't join in with their group; and moved because I was not happy with the noise in that building as I couldn't study or sleep.

~

Stephen moved into a room in the main building; the window faced the entrance. He again had trouble with the same students banging on his window as they went past, so he didn't stay there long either.

The teachers were not happy about Stephen wanting to move again but he eventually bribed one of them by promising to give blood to the Red Cross and he acquired a room on the other side of the campus, which was where he stayed until he finished at Roseworthy. During his first year Stephen brought home a small seedling. He said it was part of his course, and something to grow at home. He put the plant in his bedroom under the desk lamp. 'Mum, will you look after this seedling? It's a school project. Make sure you water it and keep it warm,' he said to me, 'Of course I will.' I did, for a little while, until I woke up to what he was growing. Talk about being slow on the uptake. As the plant got bigger I recognised the distinct shape of the leaves. I am not sure why he thought I was so naïve, but I could see the funny side of it. This would have been a good story for him to tell, 'Hey, guess what? My mum fed and nurtured my marijuana plant for me and didn't have a clue what it was.' I didn't say anything to Stephen about knowing that the plant was marijuana. Over the next couple of weeks, it died from a case of fly spray poisoning.

I remember also in that first year Darrel and I visited the college on open Day. We were there for quite a while before we found our son and, when we did, he came around the corner of the building – on crutches, a troubled look on his face. I can't remember his explanation (there were so many over the years), but I still remember the despair I felt for him. We ended up spending a wonderful day together. He spoke to other students as we passed them but he stayed with us. Towards the end of this first year, or possibly the beginning of the second, Stephen again was in strife.
This time it was more serious. This is how he described the incident.

A friend and fellow student had decided after quite a few drinks that Stephen would climb through the window of the Roseworthy College community social club and help himself to a bottle of brandy. After he'd done the deed, Stephen decided it was the wrong thing to do and climbed back through the window to return it, at which time he got caught. The police were called and both students were charged with breaking and entering, went to court and were fined. They were also banned from their social club for several months.
As the majority of students hung out at the end of the day and on weekends at the social club on campus, this meant Stephen had very little social life. He told Darrel and I during a weekend stay: 'I feel like the whole student body is against

me. I have no friends. I want to give up my studies. I want out.'

I didn't know what to say or do. Darrel wanted him to persevere. The last thing we wanted was to encourage Stephen in making the wrong decision. We really needed help with this. At that time, in my wisdom, which I thought I possessed, I decided that with Stephen's consent we would see a psychologist, someone whose methods had impressed me when I met him on a work-training day. We made the appointment and together Stephen and I went to see him.

He first talked to Stephen on his own, and then to me alone, before calling us both in together.

'It's obvious that this situation is causing a lot of stress on Stephen. He is having a very difficult time at college and is not happy there. It's also causing his parents a lot stress. I have said to him that it's his decision to make. But if he decides to leave, he shouldn't worry his parents by hanging around and rely on Mum to wash his socks and cook his meals. Pack a bag, Stephen, and head off and fend for yourself; find a job in the country. Be responsible for yourself.'

'Hmm, I've always wanted to travel,' was Stephen's modest reply.

We paid him and left. I was fuming! *Some help!*

'What do you think Steve?' I asked nervously, as we drove out of the gates. 'The guy was okay, he made sense, but I could see straight through what he said. I could see that he followed a format and it was what he had been trained to say.'

We drove home making idle chatter, neither of us wanting to commit ourselves to discuss decision-making.

Stephen decided for himself that he would stay at college. *Ugh! Even now I feel so angry.* What a stupid thing for a professional to say. When I had asked Stephen to consider seeing a psychologist, I had thought he would refuse, but he hadn't. He had decided that he was in need of some counselling and advice and had confided in this man, telling him things he didn't feel he could tell us, and the psychologist had totally misjudged our son. I had been so frightened of steering Stephen in the wrong direction that I had let some stranger do it for me. And so my son, who I now know should not have been away from the security of his own home, *with his mother washing his dirty socks and cooking his meals,* made the decision to stay and finish his two-year course.

I believe that the decision to continue his studies at Roseworthy had a critical impact on the ensuing events in his life. Not long after this, Darrel and I arranged with Stephen to have a barbeque together at the college. It was Saturday morning when we drove up to the main building, and we could see our son waiting for us. The college seemed deserted, as most of the students had gone home for the weekend. Stephen got in the car and we drove around to the other side of the oval and set up our barbeque under a shady gum tree. He was quiet and withdrawn, and showed none of the eagerness that had been there when he moved onto the campus. There was definitely something wrong, something bizarre was happening to him.

CHAPTER – 8 - 1988 - Genetic links

A person like me spends their younger part of life trying not to act more serious or mature than others of their own age. When finally they learn to do so they suddenly find that they have grown up to the age where a mature mind and behaviour is necessary to get along. So they spend the rest of their life trying to grow up.

The following controls a person's ability to function efficiently or not. Each of them in turn must be equally balanced. If any one is unbalanced then the others are affected and that person ceases to function to the best of their ability.

1. A person can only judge so many items before they fall down upon him/her.
2. A person with a realistic outlook sees that the past is as real as the present and the future is what you make of it.

One no longer lives with a realistic view of life when they refuse to listen to the truth. This occurs when reality has nothing better to offer. Another thought. One of these unexpected thoughts, enlightening thoughts rather, that goes as follows; It's okay for an ambitious person to strive to be better than everyone else but it's advertising those intentions that might cause trouble and friction socially for that person.

Knowing where a problem lies and how to make it right but not doing so is worse than being ignorant of the problem. Wisdom reins in those who think and see with open eyes then act with honourable intentions. Existing with thought is to be alive. If only you could see what I've seen with my eyes. At some stage in life all ask the questions: Where did I come from? Where am I going? Where have I gone? And how long have I got? To these I

have found no answer, but to discover that only now do I know inner peace. Now it's time to die.

~

When writing and reading about some of the more harrowing situations Stephen faced I cannot keep my heartache from surfacing. I become depressed and my heart is actually in pain. Through these times, and to get some balance in my life, I visit my friend and confidante, Joy. I have just spent two days with her and, as usual, she was a great help. She lives in the city not far from the River Torrens where the OBahn passes over, and we go for long walks along the riverbank and talk at length. On this occasion we talked about Stephen's complexity, about how unique and special he was. Together we travelled into my past, recalling family characteristics. We discussed my brother Robert and how sad his life as a child at home was.

He got off to a bad start the first year at school when he had a teacher with old school beliefs who was not compassionate. She had high expectations of her young students and expected conformity, which was not something Robert, was able to adhere to. I first learnt he was having difficulties when I was four and Mum took me with her to see the teacher after school. Mum waited at the school gate until the teacher arrived, then she really gave it to her. She said, 'If you ever touch Robert again or he comes home and tells me that he was not allowed to go to the toilet, I will ram my fist down your throat.' Forty-eight years later, I still have a clear picture of that event in my mind.

When I started school the following year and had the same teacher, she treated me with indifference. But the confrontation she had had with my mother influenced my early school life, and I would sit in the classroom and wet myself because I was scared of her and automatically thought that she would refuse my request to go to the toilet. It was difficult to understand the reason Robert did certain things, so when he was about ten our doctor referred him to a psychologist in Adelaide. Mum went with him. What the psychologist wrote in his report will never be known because Dad was the only one who read it, and he would not tell Mum what it said.

Many years later, Robert wrote a poem about his first teacher.
Mum, my bloody teacher is awful,
She's broken all the rules.
She pulls my hair and shouts at me,
And in the class I do my pee,
Because to the toilet she won't let me go.
Of me she's not too keen,
I'm in grade one what have I done
To make her think that I'm so dumb?

Robert had an obsession with pushbikes, and hardly a day went by without him taking one from the bike rack at school and going for a ride. One day when he went missing from the classroom there was also a pushbike reported missing from the bike rack. I was called into the headmaster's office for questioning.

As a small child growing up in the country I had no interaction with adults except for my parents, and on my second day at school I had found a pencil lying in the schoolyard just under a window. 'I found a pencil!' I yelled at the top of my voice, wanting someone to notice me, and I started scribbling on the brickwork under the window. Two big boys came up and held me by the arms and dragged me into a classroom. 'Did you scribble on the wall? 'Was the greeting I received from a female teacher. I could say nothing because I was petrified of this enormously frightening adult. That incident at five years old and the previous one when my mother took me with her to yell at Robert's teacher had a profound effect on my relationship with adults.

The headmaster asked if I had seen my brother with a pushbike that day. Freedom of speech for kids didn't exist back then. I was about nine, and scared of adults. I felt I was expected to give the answer they wanted to hear; consequently I made up an answer so I wouldn't get into trouble too. I thought they were insinuating that I had taken the bike, so said in a whisper, 'I saw him riding along the road on a bike,' and they believed me. I felt like a scared rabbit, and it never occurred to me that I was allowed to say no.

In high school, Robert's classroom was next to mine. Sometimes I would hear him 'lose it' and go ballistic at the teacher when something had upset him. He would throw his books around the classroom, and even at the teacher. Now Robert is in his fifties and lives on his own. His memory for dates and past events is phenomenal. He is very artistic. He could earn 'real money' with his paintings, but he will paint several pictures and then gets sick of painting and stops.
So he sells a few, bargains with the others or gives them away as gifts. Robert is an invalid pensioner. He suffers from arthritis, and has a bad knee after a 'run-in' with the police. He broke out of jail up north somewhere. It was in the local paper – he was considered not dangerous and, as he was running from the police, they shot him in the knee. Robert can work very hard but he's never been able to hold down a job. He often gets ideas, and when he gets what he believes to be a good one, he follows it through to the 'nth degree. One such idea was how to redesign my front garden. He spent from daylight to dusk remodelling, digging and planting, and the end result was fantastic. However, if I made any suggestion that it could be done a little differently from the picture he had in mind, he became frustrated and explained all the reasons why it needed to be done the way he wanted it. If I forced the issue, he become angry, and then I would have to calm him down.

An Awkward Fit

I don't mind Robert – in fact, I have a great admiration for him and his patience with people. He must know that some get very annoyed with him and lose their patience with him. He visits us every Sunday for dinner. Sometimes he is quite normal and we have a pleasant, intelligent visit; other times, he can't stop talking and explaining his ideas and extending our conversations into something 'way out.' But he knows when he is like this. I say, 'Robert, it's time to go home; you are driving me crazy.' He smiles, sometimes laughs, and gets in the car for me to drive him home. It's a good arrangement.

The other notable thing is that he knows a lot about a number of things, and what he doesn't know, he makes it up! However, Robert cannot cope with anyone disagreeing with him. If someone says he is wrong, he will go to extreme lengths to prove that he is right. He can become extremely agitated if proven wrong. It's interesting that, as I delve a little deeper into this book, my mind is awakening to other small inconsistencies that occurred when I was young, or that I heard others speak of. These things are important to me now, because putting them together enables me to see a clear, emerging pattern of a genetic link of unusual traits amongst some members of my family.

My father seemed an average type of fellow to us kids, but then he was the only role model we had to go by. However, he did a lot of cruel things to us, especially Robert. He couldn't cope with his eldest son who was so obviously different. Robert didn't need to do anything wrong – he only had to walk the wrong way to be told off. My father's pet name for Robert was 'Creeping Jesus' because Robert sauntered along instead of adopting the more usual gait. If something went missing, Dad would choose Robert out of his then five children to accuse. He would then hit him usually with a belt or a stick until he admitted to doing the deed, even if he hadn't. Robert often went to school with welts on the back of his legs. It was always very frustrating for us children when we were young. We would be in the middle of something – a game, homework or even washing the dishes – when Dad would decide he wanted some cigarettes and would choose one of us to go with him. He would never go alone and we dared not argue. I always thought he was lazy and couldn't be bothered going into the shop himself, but now I think differently. Sometimes I have to push myself to do certain things because I am not confident. I tend to shy away from some things, as I am sure many people do when they are outside their comfort zone.

When we helped Dad prune his fruit trees he demanded that we cut off exactly two-thirds of the stems and would walk up behind us and measure them. When we spread fertiliser by hand it had to be done in the *precise* way he stipulated. If we didn't do it correctly, he shouted at us and gave us one more chance to get it right. If we still didn't do it his way, we were kicked out of the orchard and he would do it himself. That was the preferred option, actually, because it was easier to be in his 'bad books' than to be criticised continually.

Much later I asked my mother about these occasions and whether she had ever wandered if there was anything wrong with Dad. She responded: 'I don't know – that was just his way'.

She once told me her sister had said. 'Why do you want to marry him? He can't look people in the eye.'

Oh God! Did Stephen have a touch of something that prevented him from reaching the goals he had for himself? Did Stephen inherit his unconventional characteristics from his grandfather, which were also evident in his Uncle Robert?

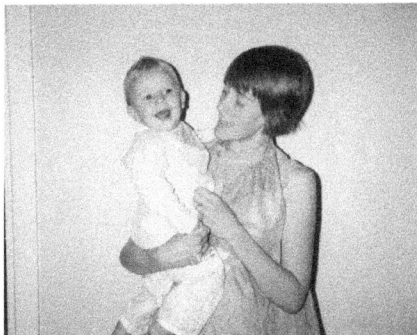

Helen holding Stephen (20months)

Stephen with the fish he caught at Waikerie

Helen Maczkowiack

The chook house at Loxton

Stephen (centre) being invested into scouts

Stephen as a student at Urrbrae High school

An Awkward Fit

Stephen at Roseworthy College with Facial injuries after an accident on trampoline

Left, Grandma Doreen Dawson with Nanna, Ivy
Maczkowiack.

Part 2

CHAPTER - 9 - 1989 - The midnight mechanic

Hmm! ... I've met this really nice girl; I asked her out to dinner, I want to take her somewhere really special. Dad is letting me borrow the car so that I can impress her. She's a bit young, only 17 – I'm a bit nervous. What if, when I call for her, I knock on the door, her sister answers and I mistake her for Ania?

~

Our first meeting with Ania was, to some extent, a disaster. Stephen brought her home after their first date. She followed shyly into the kitchen, seemingly overwhelmed. 'Mum, Dad, this is Ania.' She glanced briefly at me, and then dropped her gaze to the floor. I thought there was something wrong with her eyes, they moved so quickly from me. Then I sensed a lack of self-confidence. So young – so slightly built. Not like the other confident young women Stephen had been fond of in the past.
'Hi, I'm Helen, this is Darrel, it's nice to meet you.' Silence followed.

In desperation to rescue the moment I blurted out, 'Are you cross-eyed?' *Ugh! What did I say that for? What a stupid thing to say, fat lot of help that was.* I released the deep breath I was holding in. Ania stayed the night – it was very late and it was another hour and half before Stephen would get back from taking her home to Nuriootpa. I was fairly sure this was not going to be a short fling; Stephen had met someone who was smitten with him. She seemed to be drawing her strength from him. She was so shy that she wouldn't stay in a room without him.

The relationship between Stephen and Ania grew rapidly and she began to spend time with him at the college. He also stayed with her family on weekends.

Stephen's difficulties and restlessness at Roseworthy College seemed to fade in the second and final year. He didn't have the difficulties he had endured in his first year; possibly because he no longer had the strong desire to interact socially with the rest of the students. He was now preoccupied with Ania. Regrettably he didn't complete all subjects required for the course and for several years applied to the college to finish those subjects by external studies.

Something I didn't know was that Stephen and Ania were both on medication, she for nervousness, and he for anxiety and depression. After he left Roseworthy College and his studies, Stephen moved in with Ania and her family, in the famous wine country of the Barossa Valley 70 kilometres north of Adelaide. This decision worried us. Sitting at the kitchen table, I gently broached the subject. Stephen heard me out and lightly replied, 'I'll be alright. Stop worrying! I need a bit of time off before I look for a job.'

He had become very independent and involved us less and less with his life, but this did not stop me feeling anxious about him. By this time, Nicole had also left school and had a job as an aged care worker and was doing external adult studies to become a nurse.

Ania's brother, a mechanic, restored old cars; Stephen also became interested and bought an old EJ model Holden. It didn't take much for Stephen to persuade Ania's father to allow him to rebuild the old car in their family garage. It became his passion. He was totally absorbed in the project and found casual employment on fruit orchards to finance the restoration work on the car, completely stripping it of all removable parts. It was all pretty simple, really – well, in

Stephen's mind it was. He stripped the old car down to a mere shell; doors, mudguards, engine and gearbox, the suspension and a hundred other car components came out. Nothing was left that could be dislodged; every nut, bolt and washer was cleaned and separated into containers, and labelled.

By the time Stephen had finished dismantling the vehicle, it was unrecognisable. It was like going into a shop and buying pieces of wood and starting to build a house by putting the framework together first. It was an amazing feat for anyone who had no previous experience except studying mechanical repairs as one of his subjects at college. In fact, the next two years for Ania and her family consisted of them living in a world of body-filler and paint dust filtering through the house, settling on carpet and furniture – a life interrupted by this politely overpowering presence, which had become a priority in their daughter's life.

Stephen rode a pushbike to work during the day and worked on the car at night. If he worried about his future or had any plans, he made no mention of them to us. What was important to him was the here and now, which was the car he was building – and not even Ania could interrupt.

Most of the small wage he earned was spent on parts and paints and other necessities to complete the project. Ania had her own obstacles to overcome. When Stephen met her she was taking part in a training workshop set up to help young people develop skills and gain confidence to work within the community. Because she was very young and lacked life's experiences, he took it upon himself to be her mentor.
'She's not like the rest of them in the workshop. She shouldn't be in there. I can look after her and teach her,' Stephen told us.

He believed her capable of doing anything she put her mind to.

'Have you mentioned this to her parents? If she is receiving education, her parents must have had advice and are doing what they think is best for her,' I said.

After living with Ania's parents for about a year, the pair decided to move to a house of their own. They found one to rent in the same street as Ania's parents' house in Nuriootpa. This allowed Stephen to continue working on his car and Ania to be near her parents, who were a great support to her.

The old EJ Holden, still in bits and pieces on the garage floor, remained the focus of Stephen's attention every night till the early hours of the morning. He would get a few hours' sleep and then go to work during the day, picking fruit and pruning. It was inevitable that the nocturnal habits of the midnight mechanic would lead to domestic disharmony. Frustrated and upset that Stephen was never home, Ania in her nightgown would come ambling the short distance to her parents' home to drag him away from his beloved car. Ania complained that they never went anywhere and he was having things completely his own way. When she raised this with Stephen, he would stop work and take her out – and then return to the car. Ania's discontent and frustration grew. 'I don't understand,' he told us on one of his occasional visits home.

'She asks me to take her out and I do, but she still gets upset.'

'She loves you, Stephen, and she is wanting your attention. You need to remember there are other things in your life than the car,' we told him.

He didn't seem to be listening and I think I was a little fearful of pressuring him too much.

Ania liked the way Stephen fitted into her family He often went fishing with her father and brother. One birthday, Ania bought him an electric guitar; she enjoyed the pleasure he got from receiving her gifts. She was very loyal and always defended him in front of others - but *she* resented that damned car.

An Awkward Fit

After two very long years, the car was completed and we were all very relieved and proud of Stephen and the finished product. By this time Stephen and Ania had moved again, further away from Ania's parents into a flat in the main street of Nuriootpa. Ania wanted to get married. Stephen felt pressured. He still wanted his freedom; he wanted to make his own decisions, to come and go as he pleased. There were so many things he still wanted to do. He needed time to think.

Stephen moved out of the flat he shared with Ania and back to Salisbury. He moved in with his sister Nicole. He needed time to sort out his feelings and clarify where the relationship he had with Ania was headed.

It was during the days of separation that Stephen dropped around home. Along with Darrel, I studied my son over a cup of coffee at the kitchen table. I knew his mind so well; it was troubled … spinning. He was struggling with one of the things he found most difficult to do; make a decision. In just minutes the latest dilemma was on the table. 'Ania wants to get married! Shall I marry her? What do you think?'

What do I say? Think first. 'Stephen, do *you* want to get married, do *you* love her? You need to ask yourself these questions. I can't answer them for you. 'The words tumbled over themselves as I attempted to *get it right.* Darrel unhurriedly turned the sugar over in the bowl as he spoke quietly and deliberately from the opposite end of the table. 'You don't have a job – how are you going to support a wife? Where will you live?'

Stephen had an answer to all our concerns. It was a typical young bloke's unconcerned answer: 'I'll find a job, that's not a problem.' As soon as he made his mind up, he wasted no time. He and Ania announced their engagement.

They were married on 3 April 1993. It was 11 days before Stephen's 23rd birthday. Ania was 19 years old. For Stephen, it was days full of preparations: typing up wedding formats, organising toast-masters, speakers. For Ania, it was a mountain full of stress and nerves. She was quick to explode and everyone tiptoed around her.

On the surface, everything appeared to go smoothly on the day. But at the photo session she could hardly hold it together. To me she appeared to have lost any control over her own reasonableness. Stephen ran around trying to calm her down and fix the causes of her distress. It was little things like her attendants not arranging her dress the way she wanted it. In the garden, she was walking through the plants. 'They haven't turned the sprinklers off,' she screeched. 'My dress is getting wet.'

She could barely manage a smile for the camera. Poor Ania, she wanted a perfect day but she was hating it. As Stephen knelt beside his bride, holding her hand, gazing into her eyes for the camera, his words were forced out of a smiling mouth and clenched teeth.' If you don't calm down I am walking out.' Dispirited. Darrel and I looked in silence at each other. *Where was this going?*

CHAPTER 10 – 1993 - The marriage break-up

**I had different ideas for my honeymoon, but I ended up
not having much choice about where we went; others had
planned it for me. Ania was more intent on spending her
honeymoon in Darwin with her sister than thinking about
creating memories for us in the future. I love her heaps
and everyone else. I just wish people would give me more
control. I feel I could make things a lot better for everyone.
Would I be happier if I was more ignorant and accepting
of other people's ideas? Maybe I would get on with people
a lot better if I was more ignorant.**

~

What could Stephen have meant when he wrote these words?
There was no indication from him that he felt pressured into
going to Darwin for his honeymoon, and I don't believe Ania
or anyone else knew that this was how he felt.
When Darrel and I met them at the airport on returning from
their honeymoon they looked relaxed and happy. The tropical
capital city in the northern end of Australia with its relaxed
outdoor lifestyle, its cultural diversity and electric atmosphere
had captivated them. They both returned in high spirits,
tanned and relaxed. As we waited with Ania's parents at the
airport for their return, it was easy to pick them out of the
emerging passengers; Stephen towered above all of them with
his sun-bleached hair and handsome tanned complexion. He
wore a loose fitting tank top with black shorts and carried a
large didgeridoo which he waved at us. Ania was equally
tanned, relaxed and excited.

On the flight from Darwin the pilot had invited Stephen into
the cockpit of the aircraft and shown him how the controls
worked and he was very impressed. It was shortly after their
return that they decided to move from Nuriootpa into a two-
bedroom flat in Salisbury, which was only a 20 minute drive

from home. No one could ever have predicted what would happen in the next six months.

Grandmother Ivy at Loxton lent Stephen money to buy a computer so he could continue external studies to complete the agricultural course he had previously been doing at Roseworthy College (which was now merged with the University of Adelaide.)

It wasn't long before he was drawn into the fascination of the workings of the computer and often had it in pieces, convinced he could improve its quality. He also became hooked on computer games, playing them late into the night and early mornings. This wasn't the life Ania had envisaged for herself at all, and Stephen found it tough adjusting to the needs of a wife who wasn't happy with him constantly spending more and more of his time on the computer instead of going shopping or sitting on the lounge watching television together. Ania felt that she was now competing with a computer instead of the car for his attention. She felt alone for she no longer had her mother living just up the road for company. I invited Ania to come with me to the kindergarten where I worked and was pleased when she accepted. This helped a little and gave her experience working with small children.

It was only a few months after the marriage and during one of their unannounced drop-in visits that I was shocked to see the condition of Ania's face. One of her eyes was black and her nose was also black and blue and very swollen.
'Ania, what happened to you?'
'It was an accident. It was not Stephen's fault; I stirred him up.'
It emerged that Stephen had grabbed the nearest object to throw, a plastic clown, which hit Ania on the bridge of her nose, causing a lot of bruising.

An Awkward Fit

This was so unexpected. What was going wrong? I had many unanswered questions going through my mind. Ania had already confided, on another occasion, that Stephen was spending all hours of the night and early morning on the computer and she was lonely and bored. That night in bed I couldn't close my eyes. There was a vivid picture of Ania's swollen face and a feeling of total parental helplessness. I did nothing about it, because they had both passed the incident off as a good time to have Ania's slightly bent nose reshaped.

What was happening? What was he feeling? Why was he so angry? This was a completely different side of Stephen. *Or was it?* In the past, I always knew how far to push him and I always backed off if he showed signs of stress.

In August that year, Darrel and I went for a three-month overseas holiday and Stephen and Ania asked to stay in our house in Craigmore to save some money. It was perfect for us, as it meant we wouldn't need to get someone to look after our animals or garden.

It was a Saturday morning in October when we arrived back from Poland. We had missed our children and I searched the waiting crowd for a glimpse of them. Our daughter Nicky was waving excitedly as we entered the arrivals area, but I was disappointed not to see Stephen and Ania.

'Where are Steve and Ania?'

'They haven't turned up,' said Nicole.

Darrel's cousin Barry and his wife Jean had come to take us home, which was about 40 minutes away. They decided against coming in because we were tired after the long flight, and they wanted to give us a chance to catch up with the kids and bring out the gifts we'd bought them.

Ania greeted us at the front door. 'Sorry we weren't at the airport. I wanted to come, but Stephen came home late last night and slept in.' My son ambled up behind her, hair hanging tangled down the sides of his unshaven face, squinting at us through half-closed eyes. He was dressed in an old black hand knitted jumper hanging loosely off his bare shoulders and stretching over his lengthy body.

'G'day,' he rasped at us with a sleepy grin and monkey hug. *That was it.*

Seated together at the dining room table, Stephen was eager to ask questions and hear about our adventure from Darrel; while Ania was excitedly looking at the umbrella and cute little white shirt I had bought her in Bangkok. She leaned over to Stephen, holding up her presents. 'Look what your mum brought back for me.'

'Hmm!' He barely glanced her way and went on chatting to his dad.

This was uncharacteristic of him. He had always enjoyed looking at nice things. *Am I detecting some unrest between them? I am just too tired to go there.* I felt restless and found it hard to settle. Ania and I went for a short walk while Stephen chatted to Darrel. On returning from our walk, Ania went across the road to the neighbours' house where she had made friends with a twelve-year-old girl, Linda, and her mother Lyn.

Evening came and Stephen joined Ania across the road. Shortly after, he returned home again.

'We've been invited to a birthday party across the road. What shall I do?

Ania doesn't want me there.'

'Go back over there. You have been invited and you need to sort it out,' I said to him.

He came back soon after. 'She told me to piss off.' He slumped in the lounge room chair. 'What'll I do now?'

Ania didn't come home that night and Stephen divided his time pacing the kitchen floor and standing on the front porch watching the house across the road. It was some consolation that while we were in Europe Stephen had found a job as a salesman for a firm called Next Industries. Next morning, he went off to work smartly dressed in suit and tie. Soon after

Stephen left, Ania came home, went into their bedroom, and then came out with her handbag. She made her way to the front door saying, 'I'm going for a walk.'

I felt I should say something but I didn't, and she volunteered no other information. She did not return from her walk.
The next three days were a nightmare – no Ania, Stephen driving the streets and pacing the floor at home, searching city nightclubs and hospitals, while Darrel and I battled with the hangover of jet lag.

It was Tuesday morning. Stephen was in Nuriootpa with Ania's parents and I was home alone, when Ania walked in the front door as if nothing had happened. I just stared at her for what seemed like minutes. 'Where have you been? We've got the police looking for you!'
She brushed past me, walking to the bedroom, speaking over her shoulder. 'I've been staying with some friends; I don't know why you were worried; there's nothing to worry about.' She offered no other explanation.

I followed her into the bedroom where she was gathering a few things together. I think she took her cosmetics, a towel and just a few other 'odds and ends. 'Then she said, 'I'll be staying with my friends for a while.'
'Ania, tell me what's happening. Is something wrong? You can't just walk out; we need to know.' Shoving the last of her things into her bag she sat on the bed next to me and hung her head. 'No, I can't tell you; you wouldn't understand – he's your son.'
I had no idea what to do, my mind was working overtime. 'Let me drop you off somewhere.' I thought, this way I could at least find out where she was staying.
'No – I can walk.'
'At least call a taxi.'
Ania picked up the phone and dialled. I heard her tell the operator she was travelling to Parafield Gardens.

87

Stephen suffered terribly that week. He took the next day off work to try and find his wife. He walked the city streets, rang hospitals and had the police looking out for her.

The rest of the week saw him going to work during the day, pacing the floor at night, wondering where Ania was. He also went through a vast range of emotions: anger, heartache, worry, despair and more. We could do nothing except be there for him and share his hurt. I cried a lot that week. It felt like we'd come back to a hellhole. I have no idea how – call it intuition – but I knew the neighbour across the road had the answer. I had become suspicious when I noticed that Lyn's constant friend and visitor wasn't visiting any more, whereas before Ania's mysterious disappearance his car had been there every day. I eventually confronted Lyn.

'Lyn, where is Ania? Is she with your friend?'

With a look of resignation, she opened up to me. 'They asked me not to tell you, and it's been so difficult watching Stephen suffer and not being able to say anything.'

Lyn's friend had encouraged Ania and helped her find alternative accommodation. What made it worse was that this person had befriended Stephen while we were away. On many occasions, he had come into our house and sat with Stephen, playing computer games and music together.

At the time, Ania thought going away like this was the best way to get out of a situation she didn't want to be in any more. She thought no further than to disappear, felt nobody cared. She believed she had nowhere else to turn.

At this point I was reluctant to tell Stephen and add to his anxiety – though it was necessary so he could stop searching for her and inform the police she was no longer a missing person. That night lying in bed we could hear him pacing the dining room floor; he was churned up inside trying to figure out a way of retrieving his shattered life. I was biting back

tears, resisting the urge to go to him. 'There's nothing you can do tonight. Try and get some sleep,' said Darrel.
They had been married for only six months.

CHAPTER 11 - November 1993 - The lonely road ahead

I spent a lot of time on the computer before I started working at Next Industries. Ania had stopped asking me to come to bed with her so I took it that she had become used to me staying up late. I did not realise that she had simply given up asking. I think now that I was not a very nice person and that I was being unfair. Ania and I were not being very nice to each other any more, and I was frustrated and angry because I didn't know what was wrong and how to make her happy. I thought she was bored, but even going out didn't help. Ania left last Sunday after saying that she was going for a walk. She did not return until the following Tuesday while I was at her mother's in Nuriootpa. She collected some of her things and left. I asked Mum to stop her leaving but she could not talk Ania into staying. I felt that she should have physically stopped her, but Mum felt that she was not to interfere with what Ania wanted to do by using force. Ania did not speak to me until last night, as just by chance she had rang Lyn while I was coming through the door.

I told Ania that I loved her and that I missed her and that I wanted her to come home. I explained that I had put my name down for a divorce class and if she did not come home by Friday night then it was over between us and I would attend the class in the coming week and file for divorce.

Ania rang my mum while I had gone to my mate Cory's for a visit. My mother stated that the police were looking for her as she was a missing person, that we couldn't keep worrying and looking out for her and to come home, as I had asked her to do. Mum then told Ania to talk to me – the conversation ended and Ania did not ring me like I thought she would.

I do love Ania very, very much. I am very proud of her and I do miss her heaps. I want her home. I have had the CIB, police, St John's, hospitals, shops and myself looking for her. Her mother is shattered by what Ania has done, and too frightened to tell her husband because of the upset and hurt it would give him.

I gave Ania until tonight to decide if she was coming home and she has not done so. I therefore have no choice but forget the love I have for Ania (not ever lose, just forget) and to forget the past. Only by doing this will I be strong enough to continue with the divorce. I have withdrawn Ania's money so that now she is broke. I hoped that maybe this would cause her to have to come home, but it seems as if the idea has failed as with everything else. I am sorry for the way in which I behaved. Ashamed and saddened. I wish we could have had the time to work things out, but Ania it seems has given up.
Where will we be in 50 years' time?

A week later when I met Ania yesterday at Sizzlers in Salisbury. She said that she loved me and that she would come around tonight to talk. Ania asked me to get her clothes from her mother so she could pick them up tonight. These were all lies as Ania came around today to get her things – she could not find the clothes that I had hidden when no one was home – and I have not seen her since yesterday. She lied and made a fool out of me for trusting her for the last time. I will not have her back and swear that I am going to destroy her life just as she has mine. She is obviously cruel and heartless and very much needs help. Tough. I feel pity and sorry for her because of the way in which she is destroying the lives of all who love her. I will always love Ania.

Mum and Dad paid about $60 to have the locks changed tonight because Ania had come into our home when we were at work and helped herself to some things that were hers. We did not like it that she had free access to come in while we were out; besides, it would be a chance to talk with her about why she left if she could only come while someone was home. I hurt so much.

There's a slide show of images and emotions inside my mind which tortures me every day with every thought, memories that cut so deeply the wounds can never heal.

I have a constant sadness at times, becoming a physical pain in the chest, a pain that travels straight through my heart, bringing tears to my eyes. It hurts me deeply that she's with another when I hoped never to be apart for the rest of our lives, though I would not wish her to see my sadness and pain at what she has done.

I keep having to find things and people to distract me from my sadness, but always there is something which brings up the bad things to the surface of my mind like a kind of punishment. You see, it's not just the memories that I may bury and forget; it's my whole being. My heart and personality, have been touched and changed by what has happened. My life and my dreams have been destroyed and taken away from me. There are only two things I can do since I can't forget who I am: (1) Suffer (2) Cease to exist.

I have a terrible feeling of great loss that comes from longing to have her near me. I wish I didn't care about and love the whole world and the people in it so that it wouldn't hurt so much. I hope the years ahead are easier than those gone, even though they are bound to seem empty. I guess I just miss her. I guess she'd be with me if she cared.

Every time I go to bed, I'm lonely for her. Every time I wake, I miss her. Each day I live is like the day she left me.

Can't handle it really. Just going numb and cold. What happened to all our plans and dreams?

**I don't have plans and schemes
And I don't have hopes and dreams.
I don't have anything
Since I don't have you.
I don't have fond desires,
I don't have happy hours,
I don't have anything
Since I don't have you.**

~

After Ania left, Stephen continued living with us. During this time he was still working as a sales rep with Next Industries, selling toys, food containers, cutlery, clocks, just about anything. He would leave for work around seven each morning, dressed in a suit and wearing a different coloured tie each day.

He was still driving the blue EJ Holden car he had built in Ania's father's garage. It seemed to me he hadn't lost his enthusiasm for his job. Being continually on the move suited Stephen. He loved to achieve success, to be the best. He totally engrossed himself in his work.

Stephen had really taken this job to heart and needed to prove he was good at it. During the day, he worked shops and businesses hawking the products of Next Industries. In the evening, he would work out sales invoices and listen to motivational training tapes on selling. This was his on-the-job training. Most weeks he received the status of top salesperson. He even went so far as to buy some of the stock from the company and store it in our garage to sell at a later date, to inflate his sales figures. His reward was their recognition of him as Next Industries' (best). Although he was making very little money, his confidence in himself, and with others, was being restored.

Stephen, along with three others who worked for the company, was selected to go to Melbourne for a week on a promotional trip. Stephen decided to drive. It was against our wishes, as we thought he would have car problems. But he was determined, and was convinced he would have no difficulties with the car. Just to make sure, he took a gearbox, a spare axle and numerous other parts that I couldn't even name, along with the necessary tools so he could repair the car if he ran into any trouble. This was our son – no other was like him: if it could be done, he could do it as long as he was prepared in advance.

Then Next Industries folded and Stephen found himself unemployed – while still dealing with his marriage break-up. This unexpected turn of events left him lost and reliving past painful events.
He started hanging around home and visiting Lyn across the road; discussing and rehashing what had happened when we were in Poland and how his marriage had ended up a shattered dream. He said he hadn't seen it coming. He was still in shock.

Stephen was also still angry – a whole range of dark emotions swept over him. He mulled over all sorts of actions to take against the person he had befriended and who Ania was now with – from putting sand in his petrol tank to sending mates around to bash him up. I understood how his mind worked; he was not able to sit around and do nothing. As usual, finding alternatives for him seemed to be my God-given gift.
Whether my suggestion of his course of action was a good thing or not I don't know, but it was to prevent him causing harm and getting into trouble with the law. I suggested that he should make this fellow's family understand just what was going on – they did not speak English, and they were unaware

that their son's newly acquired girlfriend had only been married for six months. He should put a photo of Ania and himself on their wedding day in their letterbox, with the date. That seemed to satisfy him, much to my relief.

When Stephen called on Ania they were both tense and defensive and unable to resolve anything. While these things were going on, Ania was also ringing me when Stephen was at work.

'How are you, Ania?' I would always start the conversation after her initial 'Hello, it's Ania.'

'Is Stephen there?'

'No, he's at work.'

'I want to come home, but I'm so confused I don't know what to do.'

She said this every time she rang. 'I'll come and get you – where are you?'

'No, I will meet you somewhere.' We would arrange a time and place to meet but she would never turn up. This happened time after time and it was taking its toll on me. I was an emotional wreck, coming home crying each time she failed to show up. I eventually rang her mum, who was now communicating with her daughter, and asked her to tell Ania not to ring me any more. I was not handling the situation very well at all. It was tearing me apart.

Ania told me, after several times of not showing up, 'It was very difficult. Sometimes I would get in a taxi, get halfway to your place, then tell the taxi driver to go back. I wanted to go home but there was my friend pleading with me not to go. I felt like my emotions were all mixed up.'

Stephen was still living with us and spent a lot of his time backing up computer programs, playing computer games and making our new computer the way he thought it should be set up.

While Darrel and I were at work each day, Stephen would play the same song over and over, *Please Forgive Me, I'm Sorry*. However, for most of the time he was home, he stayed at the computer until the early hours of the morning. I would get up at about six o'clock to start preparing for work and would take him a coffee and he would coax me into sitting with him for a bit. A few hours every two or three days he would sleep when he couldn't keep awake any more. He was depressed and withdrawn.

The time passed quickly. Occasionally Stephen went out. He wasn't himself and, at this stage, he wasn't confiding in us very much. I guess there wasn't much to say. He seldom mentioned Ania. He very rarely smiled and always looked stressed and anxious. To me, his voice was still pleasant; he spoke softly, using a low tone. It was easy just to leave him be this way and I could keep my stress and anxiety about him buried. I could pretend life in our household was normal.

I remember mentioning Stephen to my work colleagues but I didn't elaborate too much. I kept the full extent of my grief and pain hidden even from myself. I was too afraid to let it surface – too afraid to cry.

My stomach aches and the tears come when I remember these things that happened. I would like to tell myself this was someone else's life, not ours. This didn't happen to us – it was only a dream. But it did and it is costing me emotionally to relive this again and again.

Apart from some Saturday evenings, when he went into the city, Stephen had a few friends he would visit and with whom he would have guitar music sessions. However, most of the time he was depressed and reclusive. We insisted he came on outings with us. Darrel took him to the Vintage Festival in the Barossa Valley. He didn't want to go but he did and enjoyed it. I was pleased to see him doing something with his dad and hoped that maybe they would have a chance to talk about things.

An Awkward Fit

Spring had slipped into summer and we came to the first Christmas without Ania. Stephen sat on the floor leaning against the wall opening his gifts with a smile on his face. A quiet smile of moderation. He was holding back something, maybe a secret. I failed to read him. Darrel's mum Ivy and Nicole were with us. It was a quiet day, but a good one.

It's more than six years since these things occurred. I can't help reliving the events.
It's Saturday evening; it's dark and cold outside and the heater is on. Darrel has a CD playing quiet songs. I'm worried about getting enough time to complete this book. All day, ideas have been running through my head. This is really stressful. I am thinking of Stephen. Sometimes, like now, it is so real and it hurts so much. Then, at other times, it's like a dream in which he never really existed. He is just someone I have dreamed up to include in my life so I can imagine I once had two children. But the photos are real. His smiling face is real even now. It will never leave me. I will always see it. Oh God! You know he was real. You gave him to me to look after! We did have some fun times – they were real. I remember when Stephen was in grade 2 and he came home from school; 'Mum, my teacher wants to know how old you are.' 'Tell him I'm 21.' I was 25 and thought that I was old.'

Another day the teacher asked the class for any ideas as to where they could go for an excursion. Not far from Salisbury North where we lived was the Bolivar sewerage works and whenever the wind blew the wrong way we would get a good whiff of it so we would always refer to it as the perfume factory not realising this, our children really believed that was what it was. When his teacher asked for excursion ideas, Stephen suggested that the class visit the Bolivar perfume factory. He felt foolish when the class laughed at him, and wasn't at all impressed with us when he came home.
We were the ideal family, young and fit, with two children, a boy and a girl old enough to enjoy and have fun with. We

would visit my parents in Mount Barker. On the way home we had to pass through a tunnel and the children always wanted Dad to blow the car horn because it echoed in the tunnel.

One weekend, we were preparing to go camping. The children were in their early teens. Stephen, Nicole and I used to have wrestles on the lounge room floor and tickle each other. This day Stephen was tickling Nicole. 'Stop! Stop! I can't stand any more.'

The words came tumbling out through her laughter. She laughed so hard that the blood vessels in both eyes burst. Her eyes looked like red traffic lights. We didn't realise what had happened; she looked scary. Darrel took her to the doctor who said she would be alright. He had a huge grin on his face, which he desperately tried to hide.

CHAPTER 12 - March – 1994 - Friends and foes

I was packing some of my belongings in boxes when Dad entered the room, followed by Mum who stood by the door. He had an uncharacteristic look about him, which I had only seen once before, though at first I couldn't pick it. I thought he had come to give me money, so I put my hand out in jest.

In response he replied 'No,' but continued after a brief pause. 'I just rang the Mildura hospital and spoke with Uncle Bob. The nurse said that it'd be best if Uncle Bob explained.' He had told Dad he was coughing up blood and had pain from his throat to his stomach. 'What do you think it could be?'

'Lung cancer?' I replied.

'He's been smoking about the same as the other three of his mates that have died from cancer,' Mum commented.

'He'll die if he's coughing up blood and is on the fourth drip – he'll probably die,' stated Dad.

I couldn't believe that. It just wasn't right to think that my favourite uncle could die. It's true he hadn't been looking after himself properly, but was it that bad?

'It mightn't be cancer. It might be something else. You can't say he'll die without the test results,' I said to Dad. Then it occurred to me as he left the room that he was really upset inside and that only when his father had died had he been similarly upset.

I must find a place of my own to live where I won't have the added stress of my parents constantly trying to help me. I can't help being what I am; I have always been capable of being different from others. Does that mean I am crazy? No – I am just as normal as anyone else. I just wish I could get rid of this feeling of failure and get on with my life.

'Stephen may be right,' was Mum's response to what I'd just said. 'But I'd hate to think of Bob's kids and how it would affect them,' added Mum as she left the room. I am very sad and empty inside; I cannot continue like this because it hurts too much. I no longer want to think about things which give me pain. But life goes on and so I must forget the past and continue on my own. My parents are constantly worrying about me and trying to make me sleep and eat, which I find impossible to do and only adds to my stress.

~

After six months of being separated from Ania, Stephen wanted desperately to rebuild his shattered life. Sitting on the computer hour after hour did not make that dreaded feeling of loss go away. It lurked in every corner of the house, our house – the house they had shared together for the last three months of their marriage.

Stephen decided to move out of home. It was a good idea. The first thing he needed to do was get himself back on his feet, and he needed to start forming new friendships and begin picking up the shattered pieces of his life.

He moved into a unit in the same block of flats as Nicole in Ponton Street, Salisbury. There was comfort for him in knowing his sister was nearby, although they didn't see each other very often because of Nicole's erratic working hours. Most of their meetings were when Nicky banged on his door to tell him to shift his car. He would park in her spot because it was more secluded than his, and he had a fear of getting his car stolen as had happened once before. Initially Nicky was upset because she felt Stephen would impede her independence and impose on friends she had made in her new unit.

An Awkward Fit

I saw Nicole as being very different from her brother. She had left school in year 11 and started working in aged care, always knowing what she wanted and plodding along steadily until she achieved her goals. Nicole moved out of home when she was 19 and rented a house in Salisbury for a while, before moving to the Ponton Street unit. Her passion as a young child was gymnastics, and as she grew older she became the senior head coach in the same club.

Paris was a crazy but very likable young man we had met for the first time when we were helping Nicole move into her unit about six months earlier. With arms full of boxes in the dark, I almost tripped over a body that was climbing through the bottom window of the flat next door. It looked up at me and said, 'Hi, don't worry, I live here. I'm Paris.'

It didn't take long for Stephen and Paris to become mates. Bubbling with excitement, Stephen arrived home on a Saturday evening. He appeared in the doorway that led to the kitchen. Darrel and I had just finished dinner and I could sense Stephen's excitement as he watched me packing away the leftover chicken. He grabbed a piece of meat and stuffed it in his mouth as he started to speak.

'I've been going to the speedway with Paris as part of his pit crew and you should see me roaring around in the recovery truck. It's all go-go-go!'

His eyes sparkled and his face broke into a big grin that we hadn't seen for a long time. He continued, 'I'd like to have a go at photography. Paris said he would help me get started.'

Paris was employed on race nights at the international speedway 20 kilometres away at Virginia on Port Wakefield Road, where he drove a recovery truck and took photos. It wasn't long before Stephen was also roaring around in the truck removing broken-down vehicles from the racetrack. He was in his element.

His whole demeanour changed. He had struck up a close friendship with Paris, who had no regular job, thought himself a bit suave and a slick photographer, and took his photo sessions very seriously, doing a few photographic jobs for different people.

'That's great! It's so good to see you enjoying yourself,' I said.

He had suddenly bounced back again. Entirely positive.

Wow! My heart suddenly seemed lighter than it had for a long time. Was this really happening? Were things getting better for him at last?

It was on the tip of my tongue to mention finding a job, but I didn't. Instead I revelled in his excitement and renewed enthusiasm for life.

It was Nicole who introduced Stephen to Linda – who lived in the unit downstairs – when they were both invited to play a game of Scategories with a group of young people from the adjoining flats.

Linda later told me:

I thought Steve was a spunk. We got on well and we got to talk and decided that, as we were paying rent for two units, we should share. I gave up my flat and moved in with Steve. We both had our own separate lives. We were flat mates and friends.

Steve was impressed that I liked the computer too, and we would stay up until about 3 am playing games. I remember one night when I was sound asleep – it was about two in the morning – and I was woken up by this loud *boom boom* coming from the lounge room. I walked in there with my eyes half closed, not really seeing, more like feeling my way along, and there was Steve sitting on the floor with his guitar in his lap. 'What the hell are you doing?' I shouted at him. I had to shout because the music was up so loud that he wouldn't have heard me. Well, he had thought of a song and reckoned he would be able to work out the chords for it, so that was what he was doing. This was Steve; he was like that, predictably unpredictable. He could work out a tune and play it without trying. He even wrote some of his own songs. He wasn't working when I moved in, but soon after he got a job working night shift.

Steve was a very caring person, not just for his friends but he seemed to care about everyone, even strangers. He thought nothing of helping someone he had not met before. He told me about his marriage break-up, we sat down once and watched the video of his wedding. He didn't cry but I could see tears in his eyes and he would get up every now and then and walk out of the room. He didn't say much about her, said he had only been married for six months and she had walked out on him. He mentioned that she had been in a hurry to get married, even though he wasn't ready to.

I wasn't in the flat that long when I met a guy and moved into a house with him. When that fell through I came back to the flats. Whenever I needed someone to talk to, I always showed up at Steve's. He was always there for me.

I became pregnant. I wasn't in the flats at that time; in fact, I hadn't seen Steve for ages. Then when I was in the hospital having my baby, Steve rocked up. He said he thought it was about time I had her and just dropped in to see if I had. I can't believe that he got off the train, bought some flowers, walked in, and I was there in hospital. To this day, it still blows me away that he could do something like that.

My friend Michelle thought he was cute and said I should get together with him, but it wasn't like that. By the time I had the baby I was living in a house in Gawler. I lost contact with Steve and didn't see him for nearly a year.

It was devastating that Stephen should encounter Ania and her new boyfriend while in the simple act of crossing the road. On that day, while out shopping, Stephen decided to walk to the kindergarten where I worked, about two kilometres away. As he paused at the kerb waiting to cross the road, he saw the red car. It was Ania and his ex-mate, waiting for the traffic lights to turn green. He ran up to the car and kicked it.

'Why? Why did you do that to me?' he shouted. It was seven months since she had left him.

Not surprisingly, the occupants of the car panicked; they were terrified of what he would do next. The lights turned green and they sped off with Stephen in pursuit. Of course he didn't catch them, and they drove out of sight.

The next thing that happened was a big mistake on their part. They decided I should be involved and drove to my work. The guy came inside the kindergarten and fetched me to see the dent Stephen had made in his car.

'Look! Look what your son has done to my car. I look after my car,' he said, almost shouting at me.

Anger welled up inside me. *How dare he seek solace from me, of all people. Is he stupid?*

Looking at the boot-sized dent was almost a satisfying experience for me. Up to this point, I had not admitted it but I also wanted to punch his lights out for what I felt he had done to my family.

What do you damned well expect? You took his wife and you don't expect him to react to the pain he is feeling?

This was not normally how I felt about things. What was happening to me? Had this affected me so much that I was losing my understanding and compassion? I guess my reaction was to protect my son, and a result of the anxiety and pain I was suffering with him.

Out of the corner of my eye, I sensed, before I saw, Stephen taking great long strides across the car park. The speed at which he moved was incredible. He didn't stop. I stepped back, his fist came up, and he whacked the guy in the jaw, sending him sprawling on the ground. It happened so swiftly. All the while Ania had been sitting in the car trying to avoid any contact with me.

I stood in front of Stephen to prevent him from going any further with the attack. I had no idea what to do next, when divine intervention took place. I was working at the Salisbury Lutheran Kindergarten and at that very moment the pastor walked from the vestry across the car park to his office.

I called out appealing to him for help: 'These people need to talk. Would you please sit with us and see if we can sort this out?' We sat around in a small circle in Pastor's office. I don't remember the whole discussion but I do remember not being satisfied. I didn't think it was much help to Stephen. I remember Ania saying she was frightened of Stephen and what he would do and there was the suggestion of a restraining order being taken against him. Silence fell. Then, suddenly, Stephen was on his feet. With his arm outstretched, he offered his hand to his ex-mate and said, 'You don't have to worry; I won't bother you any more.' And he didn't. I was totally stunned. I had thought that the pastor would suggest some sort of counselling for Stephen to overcome his anger, but there was no follow-up. This was his church he had grown up in; this was the minister he had known for years. Here he would find no help.

To me that was adding another nail to his coffin. For me, it was one more frustration that I had to bear. I now had to look for help else where.

The confrontation with Ania and her partner affected Stephen deeply and opened up wounds that were starting to heal. He was spending most of his time indoors; he wasn't eating properly and was smoking heavily.

It was nine months since Ania's disappearance and Stephen needed a job – *I needed him to have a job*. I phoned my brother-in-law who worked for an engineering firm as a floor manager. He could not help get a job for Stephen but was able to give us the name of the labour hire service that his firm used to employ their workers.

Within two weeks Stephen had a job. In July 1994, the employment service hired him to work at the same engineering firm as his uncle in a foundry in suburban of Brompton. The first time we picked him up, we parked the car where Stephen told us. It was 3 am and we were tired and sleepy. Outside, it was dark and cold. We watched the drizzling rain making patterns as it ran down our windscreen.

'Where is he?' Darrel groaned beside me. I was the driver because I was much more alert than Darrel at that time of the morning.

Suddenly, Stephen appeared from nowhere. He landed about a metre in front of the car bonnet like an apparition, looking at us with a big cheeky grin.

'Good grief!' Darrel shouted. Even with a lifetime of surprises, Stephen still managed to get this reaction from us. While we were sitting half asleep he had appeared out of nowhere, jumped on to the three metre high wall that surrounded the foundry (except for the entrance gate at the front), straddled the barbed wire, leapt off the fence and landed in front of us. Forever trying to find a short cut, he decided this was the quickest way – if only by a distance of about three metres.

The foundry work was physically demanding but he was very fit. 'This is better than going to the gym to exercise and build up my muscles,' he told his father.

Working night shift suited Stephen because of his disordered sleeping patterns. He would begin work at 4 pm and go through till 3 am. I believed *again* that he was getting his life back together; he had a job, and friends in the flats where he lived, and he was beginning to put his marriage breakdown behind him. For all his differences of doing things *his* way, I felt proud of our son and was happy he was getting on with his life. I enjoyed those feelings, because they didn't come very often

'How's work going?' I asked.

Stephen had come home to help Darrel cut down a large gum tree in our front garden that was threatening to drop its branches on our shed.

'It's okay,' he replied. 'But it's annoying me that the other day some of the guys came to where I was working on the production line and told me I have to slow down because the older guys up further on the line can't keep up. I'm working too fast and setting the pace for others.' By this time he had stopped, turned and was talking to both Darrel and me.

'I don't think it's fair. I'm working as fast as I can. That's how I work. I wouldn't be doing my job right if I was to slow down to their pace – it's not my fault they are slow.'

Darrel looked at me quizzically.

'It's not personal – it's about cooperating and working as a team,' Darrel tried to explain to him, but he didn't seem to understand. Some of the rules didn't make sense to him.

We had run into this problem before. He was young, up front, ready to go, and it caused resentment with the older workers who had been in the job a long time. They were trying to pull him into line, trying to get him to slow down a bit. He was going like a threshing machine – typical old bull – young bull situation. He wasn't alert to the fact that he was making life difficult for others. He couldn't adjust to different situations. There was only one way to work and that was fast this was his thinking, the way his mind worked, and he couldn't see he was upsetting his workmates.

More dangerous yet was the fact that this was due to his mentality. His mind was driving him to go at full speed. He was hyperactive, which was also causing his inability to sleep. Another thing bothering Stephen about work was the way some of the workers rubbished their colleagues behind their backs at smoko time. To him it was unacceptable. It meant that they were talking about *him* behind his back. And the problems kept coming. Stephen's uncle was one of the foremen on his shifts. I don't remember exactly what happened, but Stephen said his uncle embarrassed him in front of the other workers. It was probably trivial but to Stephen's very sensitive nature it would have been humiliating.

When I put my head on my pillow last night it was full of Stephen and his complexities. I closed my eyes and I saw faces. They were images of several people; some had angry looks. Different faces kept coming into view, it was me. I could see myself lying on the pillow with my eyes closed, then the image faded away. I then saw Stephen; he'd come striding around a corner walking towards me with a smile on his face. It was a great comfort to me. When those images disappeared, for a while I saw a long tunnel with white figures floating at the end. I wasn't asleep because I shook Darrel, who was beside me, and told him what I had experienced. I don't know why I had these images, but they made me feel good.

CHAPTER 13 – 1994 - A matter of principle

I had about six months off work before gaining employment with Catalyst Labour Hire Pty Port Road, Hindmarsh. My employer engaged me as a fettler and hired me out initially to BTR Engineering of Bowden. I commenced work at the BTR engineering work site in mid- July 1994.

This was my first job as a fettler. The work involved on-the-job training and was basically involved in the production of metal castings. I was required to use a handheld grinder and a sledgehammer to break excess metal and trim the castings. I also used a bench grinder, which was mounted low and resulted in me having to bend my neck to operate it. It was heavy work because I had to use my shoulder muscles to support and lift the metal to the grinder and then turn the body to place the metal onto the conveyor belt.

I worked six days a week, Monday through to Saturday, and had Saturday night off. I was working night shift, commencing at 4 pm and working one day 10 hours and the next day 12 to 13 hours and then back to 10 hours per day. I was forced, as part of my contract, to work these long hours. I was working between 60 and 65 hours a week.

The injury happened in the workshop about half an hour before my shift was due to end on that day, which was about 1.30 am. At the time of the accident, I was lifting a heavy metal casting. I was grinding the casting and had to lift the casting to place it on the conveyor belt. The injury occurred when I was taking the full weight of the casting in my hands, lifting and turning my body at the same time to place it from the grinding machine on to the conveyor belt.

During the course of this action I felt a sudden tearing sensation in my left shoulder and into the left side of my neck. The tearing sensation felt like a pulling of all the muscles in the left side of the neck and shoulder.

I reported the incident to my supervisor and hoped that the pain would go away. I worked at a slower rate for the next 25 minutes or so, to enable me to finish my shift. I went home with the hope that the pain would subside after I rested overnight.

Unfortunately, I could not sleep because of the pain. I cannot recall whether I saw my local general practitioner the next day or the day after. All I know is that the pain was so bad that I could not return to work. I was issued a certificate to be totally off work.

I took the certificate to work and made a WorkCover claim, which was accepted by the WorkCover Corporation. From the onset of my injury it became clear that [the recruiting agency] was not going to find me alternative duties. From that time onwards, the whole rehabilitation program was designed around trying to convince me that there was nothing wrong with me and I should, in fact, get out into the workforce and find a job for myself. I was pushed very hard by my rehabilitation officer and WorkCover generally to try and get myself better and find employment. As the weeks went by, my condition was not getting any better.

By the early stages of 1995, I was becoming increasingly anxious and depressed due to the changes in my life rendered by my injuries – the ongoing pain problems I was having in my shoulder and neck – as well as the uncertainty as to my future.
By this stage I was aware that my employer had closed its doors and that my job prospects were very dim. I was also

being hassled generally by the rehabilitation consultants. They were pushing me at all times to get back to work when quite clearly I still had ongoing problems with my shoulder and neck. They did not understand or care about me at all.

I was referred to Job Club and I became very distressed and weakened by the whole process. I was feeling unhappy, confused, angry, not enjoying life, lacking confidence, feeling depressed, not being constructive, avoiding people most of the time and getting headaches even after trivial activities such as doing the dishes. By mid-1995, I was even feeling suicidal.

When I went to Job Club, I felt demeaned. I felt frightened; I could not stand being confined in a way which is more like a prison sentence than a rehabilitation process. I used every excuse possible to get out of going. It was a very negative environment, which made me feel paranoid about the whole process. When I did not go every day, the rehabilitation officer put pressure on me and made complaints. I could not face going there; I was having chronic pain and suicidal thoughts.

I remember clearly contemplating suicide on many occasions. I would sit on top of buildings and manoeuvre myself closer to the edge, only pulling back at the last moment. I also remember at this stage being in the bathroom with my razor, just staring and contemplating bringing an end to my life. I also considered walking under buses and trucks.

My condition deteriorated so badly that I was hyperventilating. I did not trust anyone. I felt that the whole rehabilitation process was designed to try to destroy me. I was crying out for help but found that the rehabilitation providers were only interested in saving money and pushing me back to work when, quite clearly,

with the chronic pain problems I was suffering, I was unfit to do so. I had a letter, I believe from my then local practitioner, saying I was only fit for two days a week at the Job Club.

This was derided by the rehabilitation officer and not accepted. This battle with the rehabilitation department continued for over a year. They did not seem to care that I was suffering from chronic pain and my condition was deteriorating.

~

At the beginning, when Stephen was on WorkCover, Darrel and I were asking ourselves. *Was his pain real or a figment of his imagination?*

It wasn't long before our question was answered. Shortly after his injury one evening Stephen was visiting us and, during dinner, he suddenly grabbed his neck and ran into the bathroom saying, 'I can't stand the pain. I have to put hot water on it!' He stood in the shower for almost an hour.

Stephen began physiotherapy treatment three times a week. He was also prescribed sleeping tablets and analgesics for the pain. A requirement of being on Workcover was visiting his local GP each week for check ups and a medical certificate for continued WorkCover payments.

After several weeks, his doctor suggested he try returning to light duties. Stephen spent two days going through a functional capacity test and then became eligible for the WorkCover Rise Scheme, which meant that anyone willing to employ him would be financially assisted by the WorkCover Corporation.

This led to a job at a plant shop for two weeks, which he enjoyed immensely, then a job as a console operator at a fuel depot. He was able to attend most days but there were some occasions when he was in too much pain. This job as a console operator only lasted a few weeks before the company closed down. When he was working, he was more settled and seemed to be able to cope a lot better. He was able to talk about his work and he showed some interest in his life. He was now unemployed again.

Stephen had a lot of trouble keeping up with all the appointments he was required to attend relating to WorkCover. Everything was becoming too much for him. He believed that everyone was against him and this increased his stress level which, in turn, amplified the pain in his neck and shoulder, exacerbated also by his unusual sleeping habits, due to the sleeping disorder he'd had since his teenage years.

Stephen started receiving letters from his rehabilitation consultant, pointing out his responsibilities to participate actively and positively in his rehabilitation or face suspension of his income. His rehabilitation consultant continued writing regularly to prospective employees and, at the same time, Stephen continued to apply for jobs. I don't think WorkCover believed he was really trying, but I have letters of regret from employers saying that while he didn't get the job that time they would hold on to his application for future reference.

Again and again Stephen received reminders and warnings about sending in weekly medical certificates, as well as letters reminding him of his failure to keep many appointments. *It was in his best interest to obtain paid employment*, they would tell him. He was not coping with his situation at all – he believed he was being harassed; everything was too much for him to cope with. I was extremely worried about him. I didn't know how to help. He was unable to keep track of so many demands and deal with his divorce and the pain he was suffering. I talked to the parish worker in our church about this. He was an experienced counsellor, who had helped many people, and he visited Stephen a couple of times, but the visits didn't continue. I was disappointed about this. I guess it's possible Stephen's crazy sleeping patterns were not easy to work around.

Stephen was still driving his treasured bright blue EJ Holden. He was young and had long shoulder-length fair hair and a goatee beard, which made him a target for young police officers looking for possible troublemakers on their rounds. Stephen was pulled over regularly for a vehicle or licence check. Given his stressful situation at the time, he felt the police were harassing him.

On one occasion he came home really angry, telling us how he'd just driven into his car park at his Ponton Street flat, when he was approached by two young police officers asking for his driver's licence, which he produced. They then asked for proof that it was his vehicle he was driving. 'It's pretty obvious I live here. Why would I drive a stolen vehicle to my own address?' he asked. They insisted he go and get the papers while they waited.

Stephen also believed that when the emergency services decided to all use the same flashing lights for emergencies they did this to confuse people so the public could not tell which service the siren and lights were coming from. No matter how hard Darrel tried to convince him, he was unable to see that it was due to a consensus of agreement between the emergency services that they would all use the same lights to identify themselves so that if people on the road saw a red and blue flashing light they would know that it was an emergency service and give way. It may be police, fire brigade or ambulance. It was really sad and heart-breaking to see him like this. And I was in denial – I felt he was being harshly treated and, in a way, it was due to the ignorance or lack of training of community service workers in matters of mental health.

The trouble with WorkCover continued.

On one occasion, they produced a camera, claiming they needed his photo to attach to their records. Stephen refused. This incident elevated his paranoia; he believed they were going to use it to spy on him. He wouldn't even help me bring a bag of groceries in from the car in case they were hiding around the corner with their cameras.

Stephen became afraid of going out during the day and kept his outings until dark. He began using our address for his WorkCover correspondence, so they couldn't find out where he lived. When he came home to visit, he would stay mainly inside, believing they were watching our house. When he did venture outside, his eyes would scan the surrounding area. Because of his confusion, I was handling all his mail and telephone calls, making lists of the times and days when he was expected to be somewhere. Even then, he sometimes forgot or slept through appointments, and this saw him in trouble again, resulting in more threatening letters from his case manager.

It was a pretty rotten situation for us all. Each time Stephen came home with a problem, I tried to fix it. Darrel was worried and constantly confused by what was happening. He had never been in this situation before. He had never experienced anyone who was different or suffering psychological problems and this was his son with the problems. Neither of us could really face it. We worried about the things Stephen said and did. We thought his behaviour and opinions were strange, but we were afraid – afraid we might make the wrong judgment, always thinking that eventually everything would be okay.

I kept coming up with solutions to his problems, which usually worked. I have an uncanny knack of being able to solve problems. Call it a gift, if you like; which I thank God for because of the many times I needed to use it. Sometimes the solution was long-term but unfortunately most of them were temporary. When one problem was fixed and we relaxed, there would be another to take its place. Just like fish jumping in the river – as one went down, another would pop up. However, I didn't expect this situation to last forever. Darrel and I both thought that one day everything would come together and Stephen would be set free.

In March 1995, the lease on the Ponton Street apartment ran out and Stephen decided not to renew it. He stored his furniture in our shed and moved in with some friends a little further out of town until he could find somewhere suitable to live. By pure coincidence, he had moved into the same two-storey unit that my younger sister Cheryl had shared with a friend 20 years ago, and was in the same small upstairs bedroom.

An elderly Scottish couple lived next door and they shared a double driveway with Stephen's friends. The man wasn't too keen on having several young people as neighbours because of their comings and goings at all hours. The kids weren't exceptionally noisy, but the man was very sensitive and complained a lot.

We didn't visit Stephen very often while he was living with his friends. We didn't want to intrude on their lives, though often on a Sunday we would call and pick him up and take him to church with us. One Sunday, we were dropping him back home when the neighbour came out and started abusing us for parking in the driveway because we weren't residents.

As Darrel didn't want to cause any difficulties for Stephen and his friends, he backed out and parked on the road, which was in front of the two units. Darrel and Stephen were standing quietly by the car talking when the neighbour came out again. I had opened my door to get out of the car, when he leant over the open door, stopping me from getting out, though I don't think he realised this. He then started shouting at Darrel and Stephen. I think his frustration had built up over a period of time and, instead of confronting the young ones, he saw this as an opportunity to take it out on someone who was more his own age. Perhaps he thought that Darrel would take his side of the argument!

Speaking in a quiet voice, Darrel tried to calm him down so he would talk rationally about his problem. The man became even angrier and started thumping the top of our car. Stephen walked around to my side and with a very stern yet quiet voice calmly said to him, 'Take your hand away from my mother.'

I love telling this part, as it gives me such a warm feeling to think that he was so protective of me.

'I am not touching her,' he said.

'I don't care,' said Stephen. 'Just remove your hand and yourself from my mother.'

'I'd do as he asks, mate,' said Darrel.

With that, the man removed his hand from the car, but didn't move. Darrel then became angry and said sternly, 'Bugger off. You don't want to listen to reason, so I'm not interested in talking to you.'

The man stood back and we drove off with Stephen. The Scottish bloke didn't realise how close he came to being decked by a father and son. We were very protective of our son, as he was of us. He also had a strong respect for us. He enjoyed our visits and concern for him, and it seemed as if we were his 'normality.'

For Stephen, a lot of things were happening that were out of character for a well-adjusted male. We didn't realise the sickness that was going on in his mind; things were not falling into place. None of the *normal* things were happening, like marriage, children and employment.

The next time we heard from Stephen was a week later, on a Sunday. Darrel received a phone call. Stephen had had an accident in his car, which was wrapped around a pine tree at the back of the Holden car factory in Elizabeth. Stephen wanted Darrel to go and wait for him while he hired a trailer to remove it.

Darrel describes his experience:
I finally dragged out of him what had happened. He said he lost control of the car, but he was very guarded in what he said. He didn't tell me much at all, so I jumped in the car and drove down. I found his car half wrapped around a tree in the pine plantation, and noticed also there was a great chunk of concrete the size of a football missing from the kerb. Then I looked more thoroughly and said out loud, 'Oh shit!
He's tried to commit suicide!' Deliberate and calculated suicide.

He had come down a straight road he had driven many times and also, as a young child, had travelled with us as a family. There was a T-junction ahead of him; and he just kept driving. I thought again: 'Holy hell, he's tried to take his life. He has lined up the road and gone across the T- junction, hit the kerb, which would have taken an incredible speed to do so, and hit a pine tree head on.'

What was he doing going along the back road if he didn't have a death wish? My world suddenly turned black. This wasn't normal. It was frightening, weird, and abnormal.
I stayed there for about an hour and within that time people started gathering, mainly young males. When I told them to go, a number of them became abusive and wanted to know what was going on. Was I trying to claim the prize for myself, or was I prepared to divide the spoils of the wreck with them? I explained the situation – this was my son's car and I was waiting for a tow-truck to arrive. 'Go away and leave me alone,' I shouted, only my language was much more colourful. After waiting perhaps two hours, and fending off the vultures that must have been informed by a community grapevine that there were easy pickings here, Stephen turned up with

someone's car and a low loader with a winch on it. Two other blokes were with him, whom I recognised as acquaintances of his from Elizabeth Downs.

One of them approached me and, to my disbelief, thanked me for staying with Stephen's car and looking after it. He thanked me again. He was off his face on what I assumed was marijuana, as was the other guy who was with him. The situation wasn't right for me to challenge Stephen. He was hell-bent on getting his car on the trailer. In the short time the car had been abandoned, the radio had been ripped out and his toolbox and other gear were missing from the boot.

The thing that disturbed me was that later when I decided to challenge Stephen, as a father would his son, his explanation was simply that he had decided to go for a drive. He had consumed about half a bottle of Jim Beam whisky and was suffering from a virus. With those combined effects and the shock after the accident, he had staggered out of the vehicle and miraculously found his way home. That was his story, but I felt there was more to this than met the eye. I felt much darker things were happening and had a deep sense of foreboding. The last I remember was the car disappearing with the two blokes in it, and me shaking my head and saying, 'My God, my God!'

We had no room in our garage to accommodate a wrecked car and our backyard was very small. I had predicted Stephen would become anxious and stressed about this problem, so before he came home I thought the situation through and came up with a solution. I was trying to keep one step ahead of him, trying to prevent another problem for him, which in turn meant another one for me. I rang my mother and put forward the proposition that the car go to her place. She didn't like the idea at all but I was desperate to help him so I pleaded with her. She reluctantly agreed, as long as it was only for a short time. Mum didn't use her shed for anything except a few garden tools, but I guess it was her choice as to whether she would put up with having her grandson's car body there. Stephen removed the motor, believing that when he found somewhere suitable, he would restore it again.

Stephen moved again and was now living in Elizabeth South. The house belonged to the South Australian Housing Trust, which had rented it to Brandon, a gymnastics instructor at the gym club of Stephen's sister Nicole. Brandon was never there – he spent most of his time with his girlfriend and two children, and the agreement was that, if Stephen paid the rent to him, he could live there.

CHAPTER 14 – 1995 - Psychological overlay

I have been seeing a psychologist lately, and even though I feel that not a great deal in the way of therapy has been brought into play, it has been good to have someone to talk to of the things I like to contemplate in my mind. I wish I could record my thoughts in a more efficient manner so you may know and understand me and review the events in my life. I really haven't done a great deal since the beginning of the year. Everyone says that I lack the ability to be positive about life. Maybe I'm sick with depression, they say.

I'd like to walk out my front door knowing that I can be successful at whatever I do, that people will support me, and everyone would adopt the nicest attitude toward each other. That everyone would make intelligent honest decisions, which would result in everything working out the right way. I wish people weren't malicious and horrible to each other, I wish they wouldn't play horrible little games, lie and do selfish things to cover their own failure. Or seek pleasure and entertainment in another's despair. Most people do it out of habit without even being aware they do; others are aware but convince themselves that so long as they get their own way, then it doesn't matter. How can I be happy and enjoy life when I am forced to interact with people? I refuse to conform to their way of thinking and find that people end up being nasty towards me when I refuse to let things slide (people are so blind to the consequences of their actions.) When interacting with others, I constantly find myself frustrated, agitated and stressed. I end up spending a great deal of time on my own. I get angry and resentful toward others when forced to actively participate in society on a social level.

I feel regretful of my inability to face the world and cope with these things, but at least it's easier than having to live with misery and depression that failure has brought into my life.

It's the same as in a game of soccer, where a player may be kicked in the shins a few times (sometimes deliberate, sometimes by accident); the player will get up and struggle on. Though if the other players come and deliberately kick this player in the shins each time he tried to become involved in the play while the referee simply pretends not to see, eventually the player will see that it's probably better not to get involved as he is being prevented from making any progress anyway.

It amazes me that a lot of people consider themselves to be intelligent or wise with superior physical strength, though they can be cruel and even violent. They are too naive to realise that it's much harder and challenging to maintain self-control over themselves and the way they treat others in the face of bad experiences. Otherwise they make themselves to be worthless as caring, loving, trustworthy human beings.

Anyone can be cruel, mean or violent, but it takes a better and stronger person to overcome these things. Often I have watched the flow of conversations and seen how a person may search around a group of people for a quieter person of minimal popularity to be used as a step for them to increase their group status and serve as a warning to ward off possible challengers. I consider this to be totally unacceptable and refuse to involve myself in this behaviour. As a result, I quite often get misjudged as being one of those that sit back and say nothing when being abused and harassed. Since I'm a relatively patient person they think I'm afraid, when really I just don't like

their barbaric behaviour. Usually the rest of the group, for fear of also being singled out will join in the attack.

~

Last Friday, Darrel and I drove the 230 kilometres to Loxton .We took his mother to the hospital for X-rays, then to her specialist. Mum has advanced breast cancer and every six weeks we take her for check-ups. When we returned from the appointment, Darrel and I slipped off to the local pub for a little time out together .We sat at a table in the front bar with our drinks, a beer for Darrel and a lemon squash for me.

It was about 5.30 pm and I was the only woman there. Most of the men were in their work clothes, having a beer before going home. I looked along the row of guys sitting on stools with their backs to us, chatting and smoking. Most of them looked to be in their thirties; a couple were older. It was their clothing that got me. Most wore old faded jeans and work boots; some wore checked shirts with the sleeves rolled up, the same as Steve used to wear.

I imagined him sitting there too. He was a little taller than most of them, and he was wearing his red-checked fleecy-lined work shirt with the sleeves rolled up almost to his elbows. He liked a beer with the blokes, despite his feelings at times of not fitting in.

I feel he is with me while I'm writing. I imagine him reading over my shoulder, correcting a few things he might disagree with and with a broad grin saying, 'Cool! You're doing it, Mum. I knew you could. You're doing it for me. Wow!' This is when I feel his spirit with me.

While at Elizabeth South, Stephen's domestic situation wasn't improving as we hoped it would now he had somewhere to live on his own. He was not the well-groomed young healthy man of 12 months ago.

He often looked haggard and over-tired and frequently caught colds and had bronchitis. He couldn't hold a conversation for long without drifting off the topic, or becoming so deep with his explanations that he would get a pen and paper to draw a diagram to make sure we understood. He couldn't sit still long enough to read a paper or watch TV. The only thing that captured his interest was the computer, which he used to write job applications, play games and back up programs.

Stephen became nocturnal. He would stay indoors during the day and go riding his pushbike at night when he couldn't sleep. This helped him relax, got him out of the house for a while and burnt up some of the pent-up energy he had inside himself. Sometimes he would come for a ride to visit us at 10.30 pm, stay for a few minutes, then go.
The police pulled him over on one of his night-time excursions, demanding to know what he was doing on a bike in the early hours of the morning. He said he couldn't sleep and often went for a ride at that hour.
'Go home and confine your riding to the daytime,' they told him.

At this point, he was staying awake for days at a time, until his body finally gave in and he'd collapse into bed, sleeping for long stretches at a time. I believed if he stayed in at night and was afraid to go out during the day, it meant he would be totally isolated from the world.

Stephen was seeing a psychologist with the approval of WorkCover to help him manage his pain. I went for one visit with Stephen but from then on he preferred to go on his own. I often had phone conversations with the psychologist – he did not talk about Stephen's visits but he was very concerned about him and the conversations consisted of me helping him to know more about Stephen and his family background. WorkCover became increasingly frustrated with Stephen for not keeping appointments. He either forgot or slept through them. His shoulder was too painful to go out or he would be having one of those days when he was too afraid to walk out his front door.

The threats to cut off his fortnightly payments continued. Several times they carried out the threat. His rehabilitation consultant believed Stephen was deliberately setting out to frustrate their efforts to return him to work, and this is when he recommended that Stephen should attend Job Club on a full-time basis. Again the community service failed to comprehend what was happening to him. They were trying to force him into their line of thinking. Little did they know that that was impossible and forcing the situation only made Stephen more angry and extremely agitated. He now believed unequivocally that WorkCover, the police and even some of the people in the street were plotting to bring him down.

At Job Club, people were required to undertake intensive job-seeking activities and were provided with all necessary stationery, access to a phone and any other equipment they may require. How they expected Stephen to do this is anyone's guess; he couldn't keep appointments and couldn't work. However, in spite of everything happening to him, he did give it a go and attended, for a few days. It was also recommended that if he failed to attend, his weekly payments would be discontinued. By this time, his doctor had suggested to the rehabilitation officer at a case conference that he may have been suffering from psychological overload. Travelling by train on his way to see his psychologist Stephen found himself in the midst of another confrontation.

Stephen recalls:
I walked on to the Adelaide-to-Gawler train at Elizabeth South station, passed the ticket inspector standing on my right

and validated my ticket before sitting down. The transit representative immediately walked over to where I was sitting and asked to see my ticket, and then asked to see my concession card. Upon showing the concession card to the transit representative, I was informed that the concession card was out of date, and that since they (the transit authorities) were having a campaign, I would receive a fine for not possessing the correct ticket. The inspector asked for the concession card, sat down in the seat opposite closest to the walkway and explained that I couldn't stay on the train without the correct ticket to which I replied that in that case I would get off at the next station (Elizabeth). A policewoman walked over and sat down next to the inspector on a seat on the other side of the walkway, and while trying to read from the transit representative's notebook asked the transit representative my surname. I stated that she could not do that, and that if she wanted my details then she could only get them from me. The policewoman then asked me for my surname and I replied that the transit representative was in the middle of writing me a fine and could she please wait.

The policewoman sat quietly until the transit representative finished, at which time the train stopped and the doors opened at the Elizabeth station. I said that this was my stop and that I had to get off. As I stood up to leave, the policewoman stood in my way and said I wasn't going anywhere.
I asked if I was under arrest and was told 'yes.' I asked, 'What for?' And received no answer.

There was a pause, when no one moved or spoke. All I could think was 'What an absurd situation' and that I had to get off the train, as I no longer had a ticket. So I slipped past the policewoman and jumped through the closing doors. My foot caught; I stumbled. I could see out the corner of my eye and hear the policeman who was with the policewoman who had tried to grab me; he was rushing towards me, out of the train. I didn't have the slightest clue what to do. I was in such a panic, I couldn't think properly. I sprung off down the platform. I came to the end of the platform and glimpsed back; I saw the policeman was still chasing me. I ran off the platform across the track and along the fence line, when I started to realise that if I didn't stop running then I'd make things worse. The policeman caught up with me and made me get on my stomach until the police car arrived.

After, I was allowed to stand and step over the fence. The policewoman then approached from the direction of the train and asked me, 'Are you going to give me your name now?' To this I replied with my first name: 'Yes, Stephen', and asked while the policewoman was writing, 'But before I go any further, can I know where I stand and what my situation is?' The policewoman replied, 'Nut' or' No, refusal to give name, under arrest, get in the car.'

What happened to understanding and compassion? They didn't even give me a chance or try to understand me.

Stephen stood by his principles and sought the assistance of his solicitor to fight the case. He had discussed this with me and I supported the move. It went to court and Stephen was charged with trespassing only, and the two other charges were dropped. He was fined $300, and his solicitor's fees.

This incident again strengthened his belief that people were against him. He was constantly fighting for his rights and it accelerated his belief that the police were persecuting him. Stephen was disconnecting himself from the outside world except for a small group of friends who got together to play their guitars and computer games. They were drawn to his passion for music and his clear concern for the wellbeing of his friends and family. They saw that he was ill more clearly than we did and accepted him for who he was. His inner world became a battlefield between his love and compassion for life and his paranoia that the world was against him.

CHAPTER 15 – 1996 - Mum, I love you

Hmmm. Observation: when I think or read the words love, joy, life, I picture and feel a sense of loss, death, age, destruction, passing time, sadness, emptiness, and pointlessness. Sob. I've now gone 27 hours without a cigarette. I think about how real death is.
Love fills my heart and soul with radiance.
But with this love come silent cries of anguish and sadness at being alone. Alone from the realisation that no one can be trusted 100 per cent.

Am I the only one that would never destroy another's trust with the intention of doing harm? I'm lost, yet still here, I am tired; I'll rest when I die. We're all afraid of the dark, but morning always comes. I see the sun and I smile. My heart, my soul, my thoughts I searched to make some sense of it all. I searched for direction and purpose, but found it not. I looked to others for guidance and counsel, and found that no one really knew the answer.

I felt uneasy and could not hide it from myself, I became resentful at times towards those who tried to suppress my search and tell me not to create disruption to their lives but they knew not what they did because of their ignorance and lack of insight, no matter how clever and intelligent they were.

From my frustration at no answer came depression. Maybe mine was to endure and push on, making little dents and fixing small holes. It seems to me according to my eyes and ears that 'nothing is right, nothing is wrong' – it just is. Passion writes these words and love is its strength. If only success gave me the opportunity to exercise this strength. My love does not die; it just finds a new home. Now, because you read these words, the love

inside me lives on in you! Why would I want to think about death? I wish there were no such thing.
I think I just look how real death is.
I bet I'm shallow! Am I?
Are all my deep thoughts on all these various issues showing limited intelligence?
Scary.

Example: Why can I never know 100 per cent of the time what day it is?
Why can't I sleep at night? (Even when drinking and stoned.)

I love my mum, my dad, and my sister.
I love my nephew, grandmothers.
I love my family first, and then I love everyone! I pity those who don't love everyone!
And feel anger towards those who love no one but themselves. How sad.

Epitaph
Well, the word came to me without meaning when I sat down to write these following words, so I checked in the dictionary to find what it meant. Surprisingly, the word is somewhat appropriate. A memorial inscription on a tombstone. Although I have no wish to have these words inscribed on a tombstone, I do hope that at least some of the words become inscribed in your mind that you may know to some extent what sort of person 'Stephen Maczkowiack' was.

To my mum Helen,
I love you very much! You showed me the beauty of the world and provided me with food for thought. I learnt from you that I was not alone in the world and that it's okay to be who you are. Your energy and thirst for new ways to experience the pleasant things in life and the

many ways you can view the world inspired me to open my eyes and really look at myself and everything around me. To keep an open mind and keep looking ahead when I stumbled or found things that made me unhappy. You were never lax as a mum and always made sure that my sister Nicole and I were provided with the things we needed for healthy living.

To my dad,
I love you very much! You were my rock, my foundation. It seemed at times you could never be shifted. Your self-discipline and strength gave me a template to shape my thoughts and desires and not forget what it means to hold myself firm with integrity and pride. Through you I learnt self-control, tolerance and responsibility.

I'm sorry I failed you as a son. I put fingers into too many pots and tried some things that as a Christian I would have been better off leaving alone. I thought I could expose myself to the things I knew were wrong, and strength of will was all that was needed to pull myself away from them later. That exposing myself to those things would make me a stronger, tougher person. To a point I was right; I became somewhat hardened towards the world and sadly a lot colder. I didn't realise that although at times I can push the shame on my conscience to one side for a while, the feeling comes back and it alters who you are. That is where the real fight is – to do things that in your own mind are honourable or make you feel good about yourself, when the shame makes you feel like you don't deserve it, feel like it doesn't matter what you do you will fail, that feeling bad will never go away and so there is no point to doing anything positive or constructive. I guess I thought it unfair that others got away with the things that they said and did, not having their conscience make them feel bad about themselves or having feelings of shame making them want to hide themselves away. In the eyes of the common average person, more the case with non-Christians, I'm probably not as bad as I see myself. There have been times when others have said that I should not take things to heart and that I should loosen up. That the events that take place in my life should not be taken so seriously. But it's not only the events that I take so seriously, it's the anger at not being able to do what everyone else does without the feelings of shame and self-embarrassment. It's anger at the people in the world, that they can be so proud and content with themselves in the face of all their nastiness, corruption, deceit and lies. It's anger that I am who I am, that I exist, that this has even become an issue with me and anger at what all this has made me become.

Question: Are we responsible for who we are or are we just products of our upbringing, environment and inherited factors? I'm not sure, but I think this question has occurred to me because knowing would help me to determine if people are justified in their feelings of disgust and resentment towards me, or should they sympathise and try to help me? If I am not responsible, then I guess I wouldn't feel so ashamed with myself and would feel justified in my feeling that my failure and lifestyle are not my fault.

If I am completely responsible for my actions then people are justified in feeling anger towards me or ... say that I am a product of the world, that given the circumstance I have had no real choice and therefore even though the events that follow as a result must occur (like punishment for prevention), they should sympathise with me rather than feel anger (feeling angry only that an undesirable event has occurred). In other words, is it the fault of the individual for doing, feeling, being who they are?
Please be aware that this is just a general overview, just touching on the surface. That my anger as well as my

**shame, which eventually leads me into depression, occurs
on many levels about many different things which affect
many different aspects of my thoughts and feelings in
much greater detail and complexity. This complexity
makes it almost impossible to accept that any one solution
could change the way I feel. For example: It's impossible
for a person who is paranoid to not feel paranoid about
someone who says there is no need to be. They have to
have a reason.**

~

I feel Stephen's confusion could have been lessened if his
difficulties had been evident or noticed at an early age, and he
had been aware that there was something different and special
about him. His depression and paranoia were causing him to
look deeper into his childhood and wonder why he had
become like this.

As a small child, Stephen often asked deep questions:

Mum, how did I get made?

What makes me think?

Why did God make me like I am?

I don't remember my replies, but I do remember feeling that I
didn't give him the answers he needed. In my opinion and
experience, a diagnosis of a condition is very important to a
child's future. Children should be made aware of why they
are like they are. Having a reason for feeling as they do would
hopefully lessen their confusion.

I can liken this to my brother Robert. I asked him recently,
'Do you feel that you have something wrong with you, like
Aspergers Syndrome?' I then read to him what the symptoms
were, and that it was related to autism. He replied, 'I know
there is something wrong. I am sure I have Aspergers or
Attention Deficit Disorder or something like that, and
sometimes I think I am Autistic.'

Families like ours struggle daily with trying to understand
where their children are coming from, why things happen the

way they do, and why some find it more difficult than others to fit into our world.

Aspergers is difficult to explain in a sentence or two. Someone once told me: It is like art: hard to define, but you know it when you see it. Because it manifests so differently in each individual, it is an invisible disability as people can be so typical looking. It is like a social communication disorder, one that makes everyday living, personal relationship development and community involvement very difficult for those affected – regardless of the fact that they may have superior intelligence. Intellect and coping do not necessarily go hand in hand.

I have found a great little book that explains very simply how the mind of a child with Aspergers works. It is a children's book written by Kathy Hoopmann, called *Blue Bottle Mystery:An Asperger Adventure.* I now believe that Stephen had differences that were imperceptible to himself as well as us, and this is what he spent most of his life trying to discover and overcome.

When Stephen lived in Elizabeth South, I worked in the Sir Thomas Playford kindergarten, working with children with a variety of needs. Stephen was living about four kilometres from the kindergarten, so after work I would drop in to see how he was. This was when we often had deep conversations and I would leave feeling so troubled and helpless.

'I have to face the idea that there may be a physical defect with the anatomy of my brain,' he said to me.
'What do you mean? Can you explain it to me?'
'My conscience seems to get in the way of whatever I do. I can't stand the faults of others, including my own, and that makes me want to keep away from everyone. Why can't I remember things? I seem to be intelligent!'

'Steve, we can't always remember everything, nobody can. You're expecting too much of yourself.'

The knot inside my stomach was twisting tighter and tighter. I had no answers for my son and I felt so helpless, I wanted to run, I didn't want to hear this. I don't think he was expecting me to answer everything for him he just needed to talk.

He continued: 'I had a wild thought! God knows everything – maybe life and the entire universe, everything that happens is recorded by him.'

Is this not enough proof that children should be assessed and diagnosed at a young age if there are any suspicions that there could be some difficulty? What Stephen said proves he felt different, and he spent many years wondering what made him the way he was. In his writings, he was analysing his behaviour, trying to sort out his confusion.

Stephen was not smiling any more; in his face I could see the dark secrets that his mind wouldn't reveal to us. I could do nothing and I also became depressed at my inadequacy. He wore such a heavy expression, as if he had an enormous burden to carry. When he came to visit us, he spent most of the time pacing the floor. He was still feeling very much burdened by WorkCover, which was now requesting a report from his psychologist regarding his condition. The report stated how Stephen had described his pain as a mild continuous pain and a sharp transient pain; at its least it was discomforting and at its worst it was horrible. Other descriptions Stephen had used were: throbbing, shooting, sharp, pinching, wrenching, hot, tingling, aching, exhausting, sickening, frightful, cruel, miserable, radiating, tight and nagging.

The report also stated he had problems reading, in looking to the left, washing, putting on his shoes, making up and down movements with the left arm, reaching out and picking things up with his left arm, or simply sitting or standing for too long in the one position. A personal inventory assessment, showed that he was suffering marked distress and severe impairment in functioning with significant thinking and concentration problems.

Other comments made by the psychologist were:
He is withdrawn, isolated and feels mistreated by the people around him. He is tense and pessimistic about the future. He is suffering with delusions and occasional hallucinations. He is hyper-vigilant and questions and mistrusts the motives of those around him. He is plagued by worry that compromises his ability to concentrate and experiences fatigue as a result of his level of stress. He is very concerned about his physical functioning and his health. At times he has heightened energy levels and irritability. He feels frustrated with the inability of those around him to keep up with his plans. He has a marked need for stimulation and excitement and others see him as a thrill-seeker.

He has considered suicide. He reports the need for treatment and has a positive attitude to the possibility of change.

By June 1996, his psychologist believed Stephen was suffering from schizophrenia (although we didn't know this at the time) and referred him to a psychiatrist who confirmed this. At the same time, WorkCover referred him to their psychiatrist, who stated that he was wholly recovered from his injury. This again added to his confusion and stress, because now WorkCover and the private specialists were in conflict about his condition and his attendance at Job Club. Letters threatening to cut off his payments were being sent to him on a regular basis reminding him he still needed a fortnightly medical certificate. Now he was getting further letters saying his fortnightly payments would be terminated if he did not continue attending Job Club. I was feeling sick with all this going on – it was out of control.

Stephen wrote:

I felt frightened. I could not stand being confined in a way which is more like a prison sentence than rehabilitation. I felt uncomfortable being with people. At this stage I was crying out for help but found that the rehabilitation providers were only interested in saving money and pushing me back to work when clearly with the chronic pain problems I was suffering I was unfit to do so. This battle with the rehabilitation continued for over a year. Since May, 1996 I have a solicitor who has taken up my case.

The psychiatrist said that, because Stephen was suffering from schizophrenia, he was not capable of attending rehabilitation. He was genuinely hearing voices, and sometimes familiar voices. He was also feeling suicidal and taking risks. Stephen believed his thoughts were being broadcast and other people could hear them and were trying to control them.

On reading the psychiatrist's report, WorkCover refused to cover any more costs because they said he was being treated for schizophrenia and not pain and stress related to his work injury. His psychologist phoned me regarding this matter because he was concerned about Stephen and his need for treatment, and he also wondered who would pay. Stephen was needing frequent visits and the cost was mounting up. I was prepared to cover the cost of his treatment if WorkCover continually refused because I knew these sessions were helping him; Stephen often talked about positive suggestions that were made at these sessions. Because Stephen never lost the desire to make something of himself and have a career, the psychologist suggested he take up some studies which he could do on his computer at home.

The psychologist also wrote to WorkCover disputing their claim, stating that his treatment was for pain and anxiety caused by his injury and being on WorkCover. Throughout these dilemmas, the letters threatening to cut off his income continued to arrive in the post, and caused him instant panic.

CHAPTER 16 – 1996 - A cry for help

While I'm on WorkCover I feel it is impossible to overcome the feelings I have, as it is a source of embarrassment and shame, which constantly feeds the fire. Before I went onto WorkCover I had these thoughts running through my mind, but now I find it's almost impossible to forget my concerns long enough for me to start to enjoy myself and genuinely laugh. It seems that I can no longer function at all. I feel trapped in my house, unable to leave, and going for days without proper food. The things that I feel become uncontrollable and my mind simply, silently, screams out from the overwhelming sensation and all thought is momentarily lost. It's a bit like standing on top of a really high building and experiencing vertigo, where even a flat rooftop can seem like it's tipping over and you are going to slide off the wall. When I do feel good I start feeling guilty because at that time I can't even remember feeling bad and depressed. I start to think that I've been wrong all along and worry that people might think me to have been lying to them. Though I know this is not true, I still start to doubt myself.

My injury is sometimes unbearable and other times I hardly notice … though this is governed mainly by the activities I have involved myself in around the house. Yet even when the pain is almost undetectable, I can still feel the tension in my body from the annoying ache and the anticipation of receiving a sudden jolt of pain should I move without caution.

It is impossible to accept that any one solution could change the way I feel. The time is now 3.30 am. I have no money at all and yet somehow I have to get to the psychologist in town today (and not feel tired). I guess this may all be compounded by the annoying pains in my left shoulder, neck and back!

An Awkward Fit

~

It was also in June 1996 that Nicky gave birth to her first child, a boy. Stephen was delighted and adored him. When Ryan was baptised a couple of months later, Stephen became his godfather, a role he took very seriously. After the baptism in the church we had a family barbecue for relatives and friends. Nicky's husband, Murray, had his parents visiting from Victoria. Stephen turned up late and asked if he could have a shower. He spent about an hour in the bathroom. He was avoiding socialising; he felt uncomfortable and didn't know what to say to people.

'What will I say to them?' he asked, as he walked into the kitchen.

'I'll come out with you,' I said.

We went outside and straight away Murray's dad started talking to Stephen. He looked fine, standing there talking eye to eye with this older man who was also tall like him; there was nothing on the surface that indicated he was anything but normal. The difference was that I knew how awkward he felt within himself. What should have been a relaxing, pleasant social get-together was instead a very difficult and stressful occasion for him.

To be successful and to have pride in himself meant everything to Stephen. And this is why he took up the suggestion of the psychologist and, with our encouragement, enrolled in a TAFE course in mechanical engineering.

It was not a decision made lightly. We took Stephen to visit a Polish friend who was an architectural engineer and he showed him some of his work. He also talked about the sort of study that would be involved, and offered any help he could if Stephen decided to do the course. Stephen also rang individual campuses to find out which lectures and times suited him best. He chose the college in Regency Park rather than Elizabeth, which was closer to home.

I received a phone call from Stephen. 'Mum, I have to attend an information night at the TAFE. Will you come with me? I can't go by myself.'

We sat behind desks in a classroom, with about 25 others wishing to do the course. Most of them seemed to be from their late teens to late twenties. I was 48 and there was no one near my age. Certainly, there were no other mothers brought along by their adult children, but that didn't faze me and didn't bother Steve in the slightest. In any case, no one else knew I wasn't a mature-age student. I felt proud of Steve and happy that he wanted me to be involved.

The information session lasted about an hour and a half and was most useful. It was good for me to learn what was required of Stephen. We already had an unspoken agreement that I was his support person. At the end of the session, when questions were invited, Stephen raised his hand. He spoke so quietly that even sitting next to him I could hardly hear what he said.

'Speak louder – they can't hear you,' I whispered in his ear.

'I can't! Everyone is listening and they think I'm shouting,' he whispered back at me. 'I can't even zip up my bag, it sounds so loud,' he said.

When I mentioned this casually on the way home, he explained that he felt uncomfortable drawing attention to himself. He was afraid to unzip his bag because it seemed so loud, and he was sure the whole class would hear him.

'I feel uncomfortable being in a room with so many. You would think growing up in classrooms I'd be used to it, but I don't think I'll get over it; I'll have to put up with it,' he said.

Each week I made a schedule of his lectures, as often he would sleep through or wouldn't remember when to go. I used to phone him and make sure he had transport. If he was running late, Darrel would drive him to Regency Park when he came home from work and Stephen would get a ride home with another student. Unfortunately, Stephen only stayed with the course for about six months before dropping out. He started missing lectures, saying he could do most of the work at home because it was quite easy for him.

Stephen with his parents celebrating his 21st birthday

Stephen restoring his EJ Holden car

The EJ Holden car fully restored

Chris and his partner (Stephen's fondue night)

Stephen (sitting) with his mate Kym Moss who died in 1993
result of a motor bike accident.

Linda with Kailah

An Awkward Fit

Helen and Stephen

Part 3

CHAPTER 17 – 1996 - Tubular Bells

I think the world is a beautiful place that man is slowly destroying. We are slowly destroying ourselves; love is a good thing.
I just don't know!
All I know is that unless we stop being selfish at the same time, then there is no hope for us. If I do all the giving, then others will just keep on taking.
I've felt the wind in my hair, the sun on my face.
I've seen the world from above,
I've experienced the love of family and friends,
I've watched the sunset; I've swum in rivers, dams, creeks and the ocean, and looked in awe at the immensity of a thunderstorm and its lightning. Many wondrous trees and flowers and animals have I met; air, water, shelter, transport and food have I been provided with.

In detail could I write many pages. A whole lifetime's worth, both good and bad. To all those who are currently sharing space on earth amongst the living, be constantly aware that your existence happens only once. The person next to you is also only going to be here once, your existence is unique and very special.

~

It's hard to imagine anything good happening while Stephen was living at Elizabeth South in a neglected street with its tired gardens and gates hanging off their hinges, the backyard kikuyu grass knee high and, amongst the grass, scattered slate pavers. Stephen's activity levels fluctuated between extremes. He lacked motivation and was frequently depressed, while at other times he displayed intense peaks of activity. Darrel and I found these changes in Stephen frustrating and difficult to deal with. One visit he would look like he had it all together and then, like a slap in the face, things would fall apart. It was as if there was an underlying madness just waiting to surface when his guard was down.

There were a few close friends who knew he had problems but still hung around. I believe they are the reason he survived for so long. While living at Elizabeth South he rekindled his acquaintance with Paris and Linda, his friends from his Ponton Street days. A year or more had passed since Stephen and Linda had seen each other and they met up again by chance.

He was getting off the train at Elizabeth when Linda was getting on, and she talked him into staying so they could have a chat. They quickly renewed their friendship and sometimes he visited her, while, at other times, she and the baby stayed at his house. Linda was by then living in Willaston near Gawler. She and Stephen formed a strong bond.

Linda recalls:
Steve was such a good listener that you couldn't help but spill your heart out to him. Steve was like the older brother I never had but wished for. We never had a sexual relationship for some reason, but the days grew into weeks and months and then years .All that time we grew closer to each other as buddies. We were more soul-mates than friends. I remember the times we went out together with Kailah, my daughter.
People would say what a lovely couple we were and that our daughter looked like both of us. I had often wished that he was her father as he was so natural with her and she was very fond of him. Steve had a gentleness about him that made every child I ever saw him with love him and feel at home with him.

Stephen never told Linda about his difficulties. He seemed to want to keep his friendship with her as a safe haven from the outside world, where he could find peace and normality.

Linda has an inner strength and tells it like it is. When she stayed at Stephen's, which was often, she and Kailah would sleep on a mattress on the lounge room floor. Many people would find this strange, but Linda and Stephen had something so rare and good that they didn't want to spoil it. On one occasion it was Darrel's rostered day off work. I rang Stephen and suggested we come around for lunch and buy some fish and chips from the local shop on the way.

'Great!' he said. 'I'll see you about mid-day.'

We knocked on the door holding fish and chips for three and a bottle of Coke. Linda answered the door with her toddler in tow.

'Hi, come in,' she said. 'Steve's in the kitchen trying to tidy up.'

Ouch! Didn't Stephen realise we would only buy enough food for three? He hadn't told us he had company.

Linda must have known what we were thinking because she said,

'Don't worry about us, we've had our lunch and we're leaving soon. We stayed over last night.'

Okay, so I felt a little strange, as if we were intruding. At that stage we didn't know Linda all that well and we didn't know if their relationship was anything other than friends. But with lunch in hand we walked through to the kitchen, and were greeted by another surprise. There was Stephen madly sweeping the floor – and *another* young woman at the sink doing what looked like a week's worth of dishes.

We must have looked odd! We sure felt like a couple of geeks and stood there totally perplexed.

'Hi!' said Stephen. 'Mum, Dad, this is Sally.' Silence from us, except for a peculiar guttural sound coming from Darrel.'

'Hello,' said this gorgeous strawberry blonde. 'You go ahead and eat. I don't want lunch. I'm just finishing the dishes.' She would have looked more at home strutting a catwalk than doing someone's dishes.

Nobody but Darrel and I seemed to be fazed, so we sat at the table with Stephen and ate our lunch. We didn't stay long. We had come to make sure Stephen was alright, and he certainly was. Darrel and I drove away shaking our heads, but with smiles on our faces. 'How does he do it?' asked Darrel. 'What has he got that I never had?'

We didn't get to know Sally very well, apart from what Stephen told us. He brought her home only once and she sat in the lounge room and waited while he showered and got ready to go out for the evening. He asked for advice when he was thinking of moving up to where she lived in Belair, taking his car with him to rebuild in her garage.

'It's a long way from your home and friends and you don't have a car,' I said to him.

We didn't know Sally and I was not confident that a move like that would be any benefit to him. I was always scared that, if I was the cause of him making the wrong decision, things could get worse instead of better for him. It was always difficult to know how much influence we should have in his decisions. He decided against it. Stephen was fearful of forming serious relationships; he trusted very few people.

Sally later wrote us a beautiful letter describing the Stephen she knew:

Steve was a kind and generous man. One day he went into town to see his lawyer and afterwards he did a bit of a pub-crawl up Hindley Street. It was about 1 am and he was crossing the Rundle Mall section to go to Rundle Street when he came across this girl who was quite pretty and only looked about 15. She was sitting by herself. He went up and talked to her and found out that she lived in a house with about 12 other kids, which was a fair way out of town. Her friends had left her about an hour beforehand and she was planning on staying in town until morning, when she could catch a bus home.

He knew that she wouldn't be safe in town by herself so he took her for a meal and caught a taxi back to her place with her, then gave her his phone number, in case she ever needed anything. He went home knowing he had saved one person from the dangers of the streets for at least one night.

I first met Steve in January, 1997. Paris had brought him around to the house while I was outside watering the lawn. They asked me to join them for dinner and then we would go out afterwards. I told them to go for dinner and come and pick me up when they had finished so it gave me a chance to have a shower and get dressed. We hit it off straight away. I would say that was the first night that started a beautiful friendship between Steve and me. A friendship that I will remember and cherish for the rest of my life.

Steve had such a profound impact on my life in such a positive way. When I was around him I was like a sponge, taking in every word he said. He could talk to me for hours about the computer or building a bridge and I would sit there listening to him, hanging off his every word.

He couldn't believe I would be interested for so long about all the technicality and would give me pop quizzes on what he was saying and, sure enough, I answered him every time. His eyes would light up and he would say, 'Wow! You really are listening.' How could I not listen, though? He was such a passionate person with such strong beliefs. I think one of the things that attracted me to him was his ability to listen and accept people and their views and still keep his own opinions. That doesn't mean he didn't encourage people to be better. He encouraged me with my boys and stimulated them with numbers and the alphabet and just little things that I hadn't even thought of doing before. He also helped me find the creative side in me and I started writing short stories, which I have given to friends in turmoil and they have thanked me for helping them find the answer to their problems through my stories.

I like to think that I have passed on a little bit of Steve to everyone I've come across since meeting him. Friends of mine who hadn't met him thought he was a wonderful person. I would ring him quite often when I couldn't go around there and I would ask him to play his guitar for me. He would play for me for hours while I was still on the phone. My favourite song that he played was *Tubular Bells.* It brought a tear to my eye every time I heard it.

Steve had started teaching me to play the guitar, and I would borrow my brother-in-law's guitar so I could practise for next time I saw him when he could teach me more. My only regret is that I didn't see him enough, but I understood that. When we were together he would open up to me and share things with me that he said he had never shared with anyone else, but then a part of him would change and he would feel so vulnerable, part of him knowing that he could trust me, yet part of him thinking I had the power to use it against him.

It would overwhelm him and he would have to leave. I understood this and told him when he was ready to talk to me and see me again I would be here for him. He'd go away for weeks and sometimes it would be a couple of months before I'd get that phone call, but sure enough it would always come and we'd be as strong as ever. He shared his thoughts and views and dreams and a part of his life with me. He will always have a special place in my heart. I've been reading my diary and looking over some of the times we shared together and I'd like to share this one with you.

8 February 1997: I went to Steve's place this afternoon and he came back to my place. We went to dinner at Windy Point

Lookout Restaurant. It was the most fantastic night of my life up to this day. I tried my first oyster and my last.
Dinner was perfect, Steve paid. The company was perfect and the view and atmosphere was perfect. My dream had come true; I was on cloud nine. We had a window seat overlooking Adelaide's lights; it was beautiful. We went down to the lookout after dining in the most upper-class restaurant I've seen. We then drove to my place and continued the good night. Steven asked me to go out with him on Valentine's Day; this was definitely a night I'll remember. I woke up really early and rang Mum to tell her about last night. She was very impressed.

I remember telling Steve on several occasions that he could ring me any time of the day or night. I didn't know at the time he was going to put this to the test. He rang me on a weeknight at about 1 am. I woke up and asked him what was wrong. He reminded me about telling him he could ring any time, and I laughed. We talked for about an hour and then hung up. He rang back at 3 am and then 5 am, talking for half an hour each time. I could have been angry with him quite easily. I wasn't though. Instead, I felt happy, knowing he could count on me if he needed to talk.
Love and best wishes, *Sally*.

In mid-1997 Stephen was experiencing problems with accommodation, his rent being several hundred dollars in arrears. Stephen had given the rent money to his mate whose name the house was rented in. For some reason, the Housing Trust, which owned the house, was not receiving the money. Stephen didn't want to be caught up in another financial problem so he decided to come back home to live.

Moving home wasn't going to be easy; Stephen needed parents who could be patient with him and cope with his peculiar living style. I wasn't sure Darrel could be that type of parent. He cared about his son's welfare and always reminded him to brush his teeth and eat properly; he would stay awake at night worrying where Stephen was if he didn't show up at a reasonable hour. But we were all willing to try.

We first met Stephen's best mate Chris when he was helping him move his furniture from Elizabeth South back into our house. It was like a support network, with each of his friends and family having a different and specific role to play in Stephen's life. Much like a jigsaw puzzle, with each personality linking up with Stephen, depending on their needs or his. They were his lifelines.

Now that I think about this, it's pretty scary stuff. As I write, tears fill my eyes and my throat is dry. One of my hopes in writing this book was to delve deeper into Stephen's torment and try to understand him a bit better, but I didn't expect to draw these conclusions. Looking back on the last few pages, I can fit some of the jigsaw pieces together and almost see the whole picture of his survival. Take these people away, and Stephen couldn't function. He couldn't do it on his own. The final outcome of this true story shows that. I didn't realise all this until now and it just blows me away. Stephen was very intuitive; he must have known he needed a network to survive.

Chris didn't appear to be the sort of person Stephen would get close to. I was used to young men who still wanted to live life to the fullest. I am not sure why I felt this way; I warmed to Chris straight away. As we shook hands, I took in his appearance. He looked very mature, about the same age as Stephen but shorter and a little stocky. He had a pleasant face, an olive complexion and dark, short cropped hair that, if let grow, was very curly.
Chris knew from the first time he met Stephen that he had some psychological problems. He told me he knew the signs – he had seen them before.

Later Chris told us about his friendship with our son.

Everywhere we went, people would say, 'Whoa, this guy's weird!'

Then they would listen to him speak or play his guitar, and they'd be spellbound. He had an aura about him; you could tell there was just something there. It was so obvious that his body couldn't keep up with his mind. Everything about him was significant and everywhere he went his presence was felt. They'd be struck either by his height, his placid nature, or the way he quietly moved. Or his sad face and the recognisable anxiety in his eyes and stance.

He didn't do things by halves, like the time he invited me and my wife to a fondue night. He knew we were vegetarians but that didn't worry him. He put on a really good night with heaps of food.

Steve went full on with exercise too. One night he rode his pushbike to Blanchetown and back, went straight to a party, and later that morning was swimming flat out at the beach.

At 2 am, following the night of his pushbike ride, Darrel and I got a phone call from a very exhilarated and breathless Stephen.

'I just wanted to ring and tell you I have just ridden two hundred kilometres on my bike. I didn't intend to go so far but it was so much fun I couldn't stop.'

Darrel laughed and said, 'You're a mad bugger.'

We felt good that he sounded happy. That was our boy. As Chris said, he did things full on. However, we later found out what else happened. Stephen kept very quiet about nearly drowning. He was with his mates out swimming when it suddenly dawned on him that he was exhausted and wouldn't make it back to shore.

Thank goodness they had chosen a beach to swim at where there were lifesavers patrolling the area.

Stephen had never arranged a fondue night before, but he got the idea from when he was young. We used to have them quite often at home as they were a great way to entertain. We would take the table away and sit on the floor with the small cooker and its pot of hot oil on an oven tray in case it spilt or caught fire, and the fun was trying to cook meatballs and bits of other food on the end of a long two-pronged fork, holding it in the boiling fat until it cooked. When we tried to lift the fork out of the pot of oil, more often than not the food would drop off into the oil and we would spend half the night trying to retrieve this bite-size morsel before it burnt.

Stephen came home one day saying he wanted to arrange a fondue evening for his friends and asked how he should go about it. I lent him my fondue set and gave him a list of foods to use, with instructions on how to prepare them. Stephen had so much food left over the next day that he invited his sister Nicky and her husband Murray around for another fondue meal.

CHAPTER 18 – 1997 - Paranoia

I can't help being what I am; even if I decide to be different, then I am still me. Even should I succeed at being different from what you know me, then I am no different for I have always been capable of being different. We are all just products of the world.

As humans, I love to see people show compassion for others out of love. Not because it makes them look or feel good in the sight of others, but simply because they feel good when others are feeling good.

What's wrong with being happy all the time? I wish I was. All this thinking is pointless, it won't change anything! I wish my clothes wouldn't wear out, things didn't break and people didn't get sick, hurt and die! I wish everyone was happy and nice and that everyone had good intentions in everything they did, none would lie and manipulate and there was plenty for everyone. Imagine!

I would like to have some purpose or reason for living but there is none! I feel there are too many things that are important to decide to tie myself and my life to one thing; my life is too short to tackle them all. I feel destined to frustration should I concentrate on one thing, then I must neglect the others and still I am unhappy.

~

Over the years, from when he restored his very first EJ Holden in his father-in-law's shed up to December 1997, Stephen had built up quite an assemblage of car parts. The desire to restore another EJ remained very strong and he was always on the lookout for a discarded vehicle.

In 1992, he purchased an old Holden from someone in the Barossa Valley and stored it on a property he was working on. He used this for spare parts for his first restoration.

Later, he purchased a Holden panel van and a Mazda. These new acquisitions needed to be stored somewhere. His mate Chris came to the rescue by arranging with his father, who owns a farm about 100 kilometres north of Adelaide, to have them put in one of his unused sheds. He removed the motor from the Mazda and stored it in the spare bedroom of the house in Elizabeth South so he could work on it. He planned to fix the motor up and use it in the next car he built.

Early in 1979 he discovered another discarded EJ Holden sedan in the front garden of a house in Paralowie near Salisbury, north of Adelaide. It was owned by a family with the name Robertson. Mr Robertson didn't want to sell the car to Stephen because he had plans to restore it himself one day, but he gave into Stephen's constant visits and persuasion. With Stephen's persistence they sold him the car for $800, which he started paying by instalments.

It was a familiar scene: several months later, Darrel reluctantly going with his son to take possession of his latest triumph, an old 1963 faded blue EJ Holden that had, for several years, been on display in the front garden in the Robertson household. Darrel joined Stephen under the bonnet of the car in the half-light of evening. With a towrope extended between Darrel's car and the EJ they did several tows up and down the street and eventually the car showed signs of life.

Stephen spent more time driving up and down the street and eventually announced that he would drive it home – unregistered and with no brakes. Stephen had nothing else in his mind except that he was going to drive that car home immediately, and it got to the point of Darrel begging him to rethink what he was about to do.

All this time, Mr Robertson had stood by watching, saying nothing.

'It was towed here from being in an accident. We couldn't drive it home,' he said.

'I'll pay for you to hire a tray-top to tow it,' Darrel pleaded. Finally, Stephen agreed and went back for it next morning.

The car was towed to Chris and his partner's house in Elizabeth where they had agreed to store the car for him for a short time, at least until Stephen found somewhere to live – a place that had a garage, so he could work on the car.

The room in our house that had now become Stephen's temporary home was small. Along one wall sat the computer, the TV and his stereo sound system. The bed became multi-functional, for sleeping, sitting at the computer and watching TV. On the opposite wall were two wardrobes, which were also only a short distance from the bed. I entered the room one day when Stephen was out, with intentions of gathering up his scattered clothes to put in the washing machine. On the dresser I noticed several layers of A4 printed-paper. I read the heading. It was a psychiatrist's report. I read on further – PARANOID SCHIZOPHRENIA – the words jumped out at me, I was horrified to see them in black and white on the paper. It was one thing to suspect but...

He had never said, 'I have schizophrenia,' never told us about the voices in his head. Later, I told him I had read the report but Stephen still didn't discuss his illness with us. From then on, when we did skirt the issue, he would refer to 'my illness.'

Gosh, I wish there was a simple way to explain how messed-up Stephen's life was. He didn't just have one problem at a time. If that had been the case, you would quite rightly say, 'so what? We all have these hassles but we manage to sort them out'. But his problems were an overload.

It was while he was trying to sort out his cars that Stephen had the hassles with the police I mentioned before, about riding his pushbike at night. The bike riding came about because he had lost his licence for driving over the speed limit. He was still fighting WorkCover, which was threatening to cut off his pay, and was, at the same time, battling depression and visiting his doctor, psychologist and psychiatrist. Added to this was the difficulty of trying to find alternative accommodation suitable to his needs – and somewhere to rebuild his car. Stephen and his solicitor were also in the middle of trying to finalise his WorkCover settlement.

Arrgh! Unravelling all these issues to have them make sense is taxing my brain now. So imagine how someone with a psychological disorder felt, trying to get his life straightened out. Stephen felt like a failure and, no matter how hard he tried, he could not climb out of the mess he was in.

By March 1997, Stephen's solicitor had made contact with his rehabilitation officer, requesting that the rehabilitation officer have no direct contact with Stephen and ceases all threats in relation to terminating his pay. He said they would or should be aware that Stephen suffered from paranoid schizophrenia and was totally incapable of work, and they should understand how their letters would feed his paranoia. The letter asked that the rehabilitation consultant show some sensitivity towards Stephen and his complex and debilitating psychiatric problem. Stephen, now one month away from turning 28 years old, was still desperately clutching at his need for an anxiety-free life, and not wanting to break free from his attachment to living in the northern suburbs where his friends and family were. And he still was holding on to a strong desire to rebuild his EJ Holden. While being aware that his friend's carport was a temporary situation, he started working on the car.

His psychological condition had deteriorated greatly – his mind was jammed with concerns about life in general. It was as though he was in a race against time.

He continued to work on his car in Chris's carport both day and night, and the old blue EJ he had originally built was still in my mother's garage. It had been dismantled and the parts were to be used for his latest project.

Mum's annoyance at having an old car taking up the whole of her garage was increasing and every couple of weeks I received a phone call from her.

'Helen, tell Stephen I want his car out of my garage. I need the space.'

Stephen worried about imposing on these people, but there was nowhere else to house the cars. It was not easy to cope with some of Stephen's sensitivities. He returned home one evening after working on his car, climbed into the shower, put fresh clothes on and stood looking in the bathroom mirror at a pimple on his chin which irritated him. Every time he looked in the mirror it was there, staring back at him. He became obsessed with getting rid of it, so I suggested he visit our local doctor. I should have sent him to his own doctor because he knew about his past difficulties and would probably have prescribed something to get rid of it. Instead, the local doctor sent him away with the comment, 'What are you worried about? Other people have more to worry about than that.'

Stephen came home irate, saying, 'It *is* important and I *am* worried about it. He had no right to say it wasn't important.'

CHAPTER 19 – 1997 - Clawing at freedom

My own existence gives me or provides me with the opportunity to ponder about the existence or state of existence and the rules which govern it. Of all things, including myself. I try to decipher what's real and what's man-made fantasy.

I seem to be able to cross the boundaries which encompass rational thought or restrict our thoughts and perceptions as a form of identity. Look at the world – should the rules and boundaries be removed? This is scary, because even when you've returned you are not quite sure if you have or that it's just another trick of the mind or even bullshit which someone is feeding me. Is something considered 'truth' because it is endorsed by the majority? I do know that it gives me insights, sometimes rubbish, sometimes incredible. It is a very hard task to decipher.

Everyone sees things from one or two, or sometimes three, points of view, but I see ten or 20 points of view never considered by others (it's like algebra and linear equations). Even though my being, desire and attraction towards discovery are overwhelmingly immense, I fear failure as intense as the earth feels hunger pains. Fear that my physical self is not up to the task of providing and absorbing skills and knowledge as readily as I could wish.

Why can't I remember at will?

Why isn't the information there when I want it? Where does it go? Is it just me? It should be easier than this. I'm stunned at my own complexities, but embarrassed at my inability to decipher what is relevant or correct. Plus there is my inability to concentrate on one point at a time without forgetting the others or getting confused trying to remember them all.

~

Living with Stephen was almost magnetic. He was here but he wasn't. There was an air of mystery about him. Without our realising it, something about him had changed over the years; a dark cloud hovered over him; he was a quiet, foreboding yet determined figure, never showing any anger, just hypnotic determination that we were powerless to resist simply because he was our son and we knew that challenging him would have no effect. His mind was set with his own views and determinations.

It was May 1997. Stephen's wisdom tooth was giving him a lot of pain. He had made several dental appointments but hadn't turned up for any of them. One morning, he awoke in excruciating pain. I took him to an emergency appointment with the dentist, where we learnt that the pulp was exposed and the tooth needed extracting. Stephen's tolerance of pain was very low and the first lot of injections didn't work, so he was given more. Even then, he felt the tooth being pulled out.

Stephen had worked himself into quite a state, and when I arrived to take him home he was highly anxious.

'I'll catch an infection; the stuff they used to rinse out my mouth wasn't sterile,' he groaned.

'Stephen, that's not true. You can't catch an infection from the mouthwash,'

I tried unsuccessfully to reassure him.

'The air is getting to my tooth every time I open my mouth to talk, and there are germs everywhere.'

He had me stop the car several times during the 20 minute journey home so he could spit the blood out of his mouth, and he kept talking about needing sterile dressings to put on the place where his tooth had been pulled out so it wouldn't become infected. I could feel his anxiety; he was tense and so was I. He insisted I call at the chemist to get several sterile dressings and some salt-water solution to rinse his mouth out.

That night he slept propped up on pillows and the next morning was still in agony. I gave him some painkillers, which he said didn't work.

The following morning, he again woke in pain and I gave him two Panadol. He said it wasn't enough and took two more. He was pacing the floor between his bedroom and the bathroom, which was opposite, looking in the mirror at the gap where his tooth had been. He believed the dentist had left a piece of tooth behind, so back to the dentist we went a couple of days later. Yes, a bit of tooth was still there but it would work itself out, the dentist said. At home again, Stephen kept looking in the mirror at the hole in his gum, picking at it and hoping to remove the piece of tooth. In vain, I tried to stop him. By the end of the week what he feared most came to pass; he had an infection and the pain was unbearable.

I drove Stephen to our local medical clinic where he went in alone to see the doctor on duty, a young female locum. He emerged several minutes later.
'The doctor wants to talk to you,' he said to me. The locum explained.
'Because he is in such pain I've given him morphine tablets and an antibiotic. If he should start acting strangely, you should take him immediately to the hospital.'
I agreed, of course, though how I could have dragged a 28 year-old man, who was acting strangely, to the hospital is beyond me. I'm just glad it never came to that, although I felt that an outburst less than a fortnight later was related to this medication.

By this stage I had become so attuned to Stephen's sensitivities that I could predict his reaction to things, which made me choose my words very carefully. Not because I was scared of him, but because every time he became stressed so did I. His pain became my pain, and I frantically searched for ways to help him.

It took several weeks, but Stephen's tooth gradually settled. During this time, he continued working on building his car in Chris's shed, sometimes staying there all night. He was coming and going so much that we couldn't keep track of his whereabouts.

One Saturday night, not long after having his wisdom tooth removed, Stephen went into the city, as he often did. When he didn't come home that night, I wondered where he was but wasn't too concerned because he didn't always let us know if he was staying out. However, when he didn't appear on Sunday night, we started to worry.

On Monday morning at two o'clock the phone rang. Darrel answered and it was Stephen. He was in the city lock-up, and wanted Darrel to go to the local police station and pay his fine of $200 dollars. Darrel was not happy as he had to get up for work at six o'clock. A feeling of dread washed over me as I sat on the bed.

'I'll pay the fine and come and get you,' said Darrel.

'No, just pay the fine,' said Stephen.

'Then get a taxi home.'

'I'm not coming home straight away,' Stephen said.

'If you're not coming straight home, you can stay there.'

I couldn't stand the pressure any longer; I yanked the phone away from Darrel. I could see what Darrel was saying; he was worried about Stephen and knew he was safe where he was. But this approach wasn't working. It never had with our son. I could hear Stephen taking deep breaths through the phone. He was fuming.

'He can't tell me what to do,' he bellowed at me. 'I can't stay here. He knows I have a condition.'

'Stephen, we are worried about your safety,' I said. 'Get a taxi home and we'll pay for it.'

The answer was still 'No'.

Perhaps I should have gone by myself and paid the money, but I was also worried about his safety and chose not to do anything until later that morning. Maybe it was the wrong choice. I was haunted for the remainder of the night by the decision not to pay the fine immediately. I handed the phone back to Darrel, who spoke to the police officer who acknowledged that Stephen had a problem – Stephen was pacing the cell floor and talking to himself. I spent the rest of the night watching the clock.

At 7.15 that morning, I went to the nearest police station and paid the fine. Stephen was released straight away. But he did not come home until late that night, and he was furious with Darrel and refused to talk to him.

I expected him to be angry with me as well, but he wasn't. He stayed in his room throughout the next week and did not communicate with his father.

As a family, we had had the odd disagreement, but never arguments. If Stephen lost control, his anger was aimed at other people who he felt had let him down. Stephen had a bottle of whisky in his room, and I guess it was a way of breaking the ice when Darrel asked if he could have a drink.

I was often in Stephen's room. I would go and sit with him for a while or talk to him about something that had happened. On this evening, he was particularly quiet and solemn. Darrel came in and my anxiety rose immediately. Although he hadn't said, I knew that Stephen was still furious with his dad for the police station incident.

'Can I have a drink of your whisky?' Darrel asked.

'No! Leave me alone.'

'You won't give your dear old dad a drink?'

'Go away!'

Darrel failed to read the signs, but I knew Stephen had reached his coping limit. I edged out of the room and took Darrel with me, consciously putting my body between him and Stephen's door.

'Darrel, keep out. Stop it. Leave him alone,' I whispered, at the same time laying my hands on his chest. Darrel brushed me aside; he wanted to mend the relationship with his son.' You won't give me a drink!'

These words were all it took to release Stephen's pent-up anger. Not just anger at the situation, but what appeared to be an exploding time bomb. All the craziness he felt seemed to be unleashed. He clawed at Darrel with his fingers, making red tracks down his father's face as he gathered the flesh under his fingernails. He pushed Darrel onto the bed, screaming at him. It was destroying me, seeing my son attacking his father. Dodging Stephen's frantically waving arms, I wedged my body between them. Relying on the protective instinct Stephen had for my safety, I challenged that unleashed anger and frustration that was lurking within him. This was not Stephen. Something had taken hold of him. We were all in shock. There had never been any physical aggression before. Even now, he didn't punch or hit in any way. He just kept repeating that heart-wrenching statement, 'Leave me alone; leave me alone!'

He stopped. He headed for the front door and, as he wrenched open the screen, he said, 'I can't live here any more.'

'Love you,' Darrel called after him.

'I love you, too,' was Stephen's reply.

This incident did not create a rift between them but I knew instinctively that the hurt they had caused to each other would be there, although neither would talk about it again. Stephen only stayed with us for another two days. He moved his things temporarily into Chris's house in Elizabeth North, five kilometres from home.

It's a Saturday evening in January 2003. I have just returned home from Loxton after taking Darrel's mum Ivy for her regular three-monthly check-up. Ivy and I were both so strongly connected to Stephen that just my being there triggers memories.

An Awkward Fit

His presence is everywhere. I feel sad; I know she desperately wants to include him in our conversations. Darrel and I do this constantly, but my feelings are still so raw I cannot get into a conversation with Mum about him. I should, I know. Her children are her life and she says she prays each night for us and asks God to look after our sons Bob and Stephen .You would think I would understand and share with her since we have both lost our sons. Darrel and our daughter, Nicky, have lost their only brothers. Grief is not like that, though; it doesn't have an ordered agenda.

'My roses were beautiful this year,' she said. 'I wish Stevie could see them. He planted them for me. My trees on the footpath need pruning, Stevie used to come and do them for me every year.'
'Yes, I know,' is all I could say. 'Can we talk about something else?' I know I would cry if I let her keep talking about him. I hope one day I can.

Mum adores me. I swear that if Darrel and I ever broke up she would blame him.
I think it amuses him that she feels this way because he knows our marriage is strong and the prospect of our going our separate ways seems impossible. I often feel more comfortable and at peace when I am alone, especially driving through the Riverland where I grew up and where Stephen spent the last part of his life. Today, driving home from Loxton, my thoughts were with Stephen and how I could produce a meaningful book with his personality filtering through. As I often do, I imagined seeing the stunning scenery through Stephen's eyes on one of his many trips home. There was the river to my right, the surface shimmering like glitter, and the graceful branches of the dead gum trees in the water stretching like arms towards the sky. I am moved by the beauty of nature, just as Stephen was. Today, thinking of him while focusing on these images, I could feel a spiritual link with him.

I felt the same connection last night as I watched a film on television. Stephen showed tremendous compassion for others, a trait that was exhibited by the characters in this movie. They showed such a deep commitment to a man they had known for such a short time that it made me ask: Why didn't I have it within me to give my life to my son? The film was based on a true story of a man jailed for life for murders he did not commit. The only way he felt he could survive his life sentence was to condition himself to believe he didn't need anyone or anything. He didn't mix with the other prisoners; he read countless books and wrote his memoirs.

One day a young boy, perhaps 11 or 12, who was being taught to read by three university students with whom he lived, came across the memoirs in a library .The boy believed in his innocence and wrote to the man, whom I shall call 'Ben' because I have forgotten his name. The letter touched Ben's heart; the boy had managed to penetrate the shield he had built around himself. They began corresponding.

After a while, the student visited Ben and, over a number of visits, they formed a special bond. Ben appealed his sentence and as each bid failed he appealed again, finding hope in the belief the boy and his tutors, with whom he had by now become acquainted, had in him. Finally, all avenues of appeal were exhausted. Ben was depressed and asked his friends to stop visiting. Several weeks passed. Then they phoned and asked him to look out the window. It was night-time and there, in the opposite apartment block, he saw a light flashing on and off.
'Can you see the light, Ben?' they asked. 'We're here for you. We have put our lives on hold and moved in so we can be near you. We are going to fight for you, we are going to stay here till you are free.'

The rest of the movie is not important. What is important is they dedicated their lives to saving this man, not so much from prison but from himself. They gave him a reason to hope. Why aren't we ready to give like this, to save one another? Even Christians have a Saviour; that's what keeps them believing in Eternal Life .Are we afraid to lose our material life? Do we value it more than saving another's life?

In mid-June 1997 Stephen's case for WorkCover was finalised and he was awarded one year's salary and signed a form stating he would not claim WorkCover or any other payments for one year. He was given the name of a financial advisor, but giving Stephen the money was like giving Dracula the keys to the blood bank.

By September 1997, when he paid the solicitor and other expenses, Stephen received about two-thirds of a year's salary. He felt he had been treated badly, but he felt so degraded and depressed from his WorkCover dealings that he just wanted 'out' so he could start living again.

It was a strange and sensitive situation. By now, Stephen trusted very few people. He worried about the payout money, but would not go to a financial advisor as he felt he'd be ripped off. With no previous experience with financial advisors I was in no position to be reassuring enough to convince him to go. I also never totally accepted that Stephen was as ill, as I now know he was. There were times when he was very rational and sensible – and he was my son, so I was in denial, believing he would get better. I clung on to every moment he seemed okay. These times of normality told me he would be fine. Every time something positive happened I told myself: *He is getting better, he will be okay.*

It was also around this time that the part-sale of Telstra went through and Stephen bought two thousand shares as an investment. He was proud that he'd made a positive decision to invest for the future. Even with his underlying death wishes, he continually made future plans. One day, he came home from shopping with five pairs of his favourite black jeans, five shirts, several pairs of socks and jocks and three pairs of sneakers. He also bought a large quantity of non-perishable foods. He was afraid of running out of money and figured if he stocked up on his needs, they would last him until he was able to go to work or go on unemployment benefits.

He was overly generous, but we couldn't persuade him to be otherwise. When our wedding anniversary was coming up, he and Nicky wanted to do something special. They surprised us with a limo ride and a weekend at an expensive seaside motel. Stephen also wanted to repay the kindness shown to him by my youngest sister and her husband. Joylene was one of his favourite people and only six years older than him. They saw a lot of each other as they often went out together socially. He used to laugh because she asked him not to call her Aunty Joy in public and got mad at him if he did. As a thank you, he hired a limousine and took them to the Mount Lofty restaurant for dinner.

Restoring cars remained Stephen's passion. What am I saying? It was more than that: it was now his life. It consumed his thoughts, his time and his money, including the proceeds of his WorkCover payout. This latest restoration job would be all that the other one wasn't. It would be in beautiful soft two-tone cream and coffee, colours I suggested when we first talked about it. I had decided a long time ago that I would not discourage him building another car because that would only make him feel that he was again making the wrong decisions. At present, his quality of life was more important than striving for success. The restoration was going to be done properly and totally by Stephen. He wouldn't send it to a garage to have the rust cut out and new pieces of metal welded in.

He used his money to buy expensive equipment including an oxy welder and a mig welder. I carefully suggested he wait until he was living somewhere more suitable with a garage where he would be free to work on the car without the worry of having to rely on friends. But he was adamant; he would start work straight away.

Most of the work was planned very well. He took extra time and care to label everything meticulously as he dismantled it; nuts and bolts, globes and washers were carefully cleaned, wrapped in paper, labelled and stored in small tins. The doors, seats, tyres, etc, were placed in separate piles. Stephen had collected several identical parts from other cars of the same model so he could work out which piece was the best fit.

Stephen easily made friends with Gordon, our next-door neighbour, a truck driver who shared his interest in cars. Gordon repaired his own vehicles and any others that ended up in his backyard; he could never say no to a mate. During the period he was living at home, Stephen spent quite a bit of time next door getting help with mechanical repairs.
He also needed a car to get around in and Gordon had a 1979 Holden Kingswood, which he offered to Stephen for $1800. He trusted Gordon and knew it would be reliable so he bought it, but he told us later he had hoped to buy a better one.

The Robertsons' EJ Holden, which was now Stephen's, had been in Chris's carport for four months and Stephen was there day and night. He was polite and kept out of everyone's way and was mainly in the carport at the side of the house, which had a roller-door on the front. To completely enclose it, he draped black plastic on the remaining side and end. Stephen slept in his car and would come home for a shower and clean clothes, have something to eat, and then head back again. After two weeks of this routine, he came home with his right-hand knuckles split and bleeding.

It transpired Chris's girlfriend was getting tired of Stephen's constant presence and asked if he would not come round so often. He was so angry he lost control and smashed his fist against the wall. As a rule, Stephen never exploded at anyone; he would vent his frustration when no one was around. However, this time he was so upset he could not contain himself.

He believed if someone said it was alright to do something they shouldn't change their mind. All he could see was that his friends had broken an agreement. I tried to explain that they needed their privacy, but he couldn't see it. He said he kept out of their way, never imposed on them, and could see no reason for the change of plans.

He ended up sorting out the disagreement. Chris's partner had borrowed some money from Stephen and couldn't afford to pay it back, so he agreed to pay rent each week, which was to be taken out of the money she owed. He also agreed to work on his car just six days a week and take Sundays off.
Stephen made arrangements to have the body of the car he was restoring dipped in an acid bath to strip off the old paint. Gordon offered to tow the car and trailer with his truck.

Gordon recalls:
Stephen had given the workshop the car body measurements to make sure it would fit in the container. We dropped off the car parts and they said it would be ready in about a week. When we drove up a week later the job hadn't been done. Stephen exploded – he went ballistic. He changed into a different person. He shouted at them, kicked and threw things; he was about to demolish the workshop. I managed to calm him down, and got him to sit with me and talk about it and work things out. Between the guy saying they hadn't yet done the job and Stephen losing it, there wouldn't have been enough time to click my fingers. I'd never seen him like this before. I quickly stepped in and told Steve I would sort it out.
I told them, 'Hey! You don't change your mind, you don't go back on your word, mate.'

'And who are you?' the guy asked.

I said, 'I'm a truckie and his mate.'

By this time, the blokes in the workshop had gone off for lunch, and Steve was a little calmer, so we were able to talk about what to do. Then we sat and waited for them to come back. They agreed to dip the parts, at a cost of $450. Steve didn't want the body primed, which would have protected it from surface rusting. That would have cost another $300 and he was able to do that himself. However, he didn't realise how quickly it would rust and the priming would need to be done almost straight away. We left the car at the workshop and picked it up a week later.

CHAPTER 20 – 1997 - Red Centre tour

I desire an opportunity to be presented to me where I may make a considerable positive input into this life and our lifestyles, to make all people and myself happy.
I wish to be able to love without pain or loss.
I would like to live life without fear.
I would like to have a body without a rash, without mental side effects.
I wanna drink,
I wanna smoke,
I wanna make love,
I wanna skydive,
I want a permanent friend to have by choice and enjoy it!
I wish there was a glimmer of hope that I could cheat death!
I wish I had a reason to continue.

~

I was forever planning and solving problems. It was 6.30 am. I woke up feeling positive. My mind had been busy again, I had a great idea. It would work; *it had to work.* I turned over and nudged Darrel in the ribs.

'Darrel! Wake up! I've got a great idea.'

'What? Do you know what time it is?' Darrel grumbled, and half opened his eyes to look at the bedside clock.

'Yes, I know, but I have to tell you. I have come up with a fantastic idea. It's a really good one.' By this time, I had the bedside lamp on and was leaning over Darrel, trying to wake him up enough to enlighten him with my thoughts.

We had been booked for several months to go on a seven-day bus tour to central Australia and the company was still advertising the trip. I thought that maybe it would be good for Stephen, also. It would get him away from everything – he'd just sit on a bus and relax. He would love it. I was sure this was the answer. Darrel agreed with me.

I rang and invited him. When I hung up the phone, I wondered if I'd done the right thing. He had hesitated, saying he had to work on his car before it started rusting, but he would think about it. After talking it over with his mate, Chris, he said the car could wait, and agreed to come.

There is always something hopeful and exciting about a fresh new day.

It was 6.45 am and the October sun was just starting to creep over the house as we waited for the chauffeur-driven van to take us to the bus depot in the city, to begin our holiday. Stephen was living part of the time with us and the rest at Chris's house. Last evening he had slept at our place, to be ready on time for the trip. Without warning, Stephen grabbed the keys to the shed.

'Come and see the new compressor I bought – it's in the shed.'

Our transport arrived at the same time.

'Stephen, our ride is here! We can't keep him waiting. Can we look at it when we come back?'

This can't be happening – not now.

As the driver waited by the van, I struggled out with our luggage, hoping to fill in the time it would take for Darrel to do justice to Stephen's demand. It was useless for Darrel to refuse. When Stephen was in this state, doing whatever came to mind at that very instant, he failed to see the reason anyone would be put out. Fifteen minutes later, when he was ready to go, he sat up front with the driver, chatting away happily while Darrel and I sat in the back, totally stunned at the instantaneous change in him.

Arriving at the Adelaide bus terminal, we were introduced to our bus driver, Joe. I quickly took in our fellow passengers. With a few exceptions, including Darrel and myself, the passengers were well over 60. I wondered how Stephen would react to this, but he headed for an empty seat at the back, without appearing to notice he was amongst an ageing population.

Two hours into our journey, at Crystal Brook, three new passengers joined us. Tom and Elaine, in their sixties, were visiting from Manchester in England with Elaine's mother. Alice was an amazing 90-year-old, one of those fairytale grannies with curly grey hair, permanent smile, and a sweet disposition that captivated all who came in contact with her.

On the trip, Elaine and her mother shared a room; Tom shared with Stephen. I am sure God sent an angel to watch over the three of us on this trip, in the form of this large Pommy bloke with a heart of gold. Tom and Stephen clicked straight away and developed a powerful friendship over the seven-day trip.

Solidly built with grey-white hair, Tom was as tall as Stephen. He was a bit of an artist, with a pad on hand throughout the trip, sketching the scenery. On odd occasions, he took out his watercolours to paint his work.

The two of them often shared a quiet Jack Daniel's in their room at night.

Tom wasn't fazed by any of Stephen's night-time wanderings or his odd sleep patterns. He warmed to him straight away, accepting him for who he was. He even woke him in the mornings and made sure he was out of bed on time.

At our first stop, at the township of Woomera, we pulled in at a park with a museum display of discarded rockets and equipment from the Woomera rocket range, established in 1947 as a joint venture between Britain and Australia .We were all in fine spirits and Darrel wanted to capture the moment on video. The bus driver gave us 45 minutes to look around.

'Hey, Lofty, come and stand next to Mum,' Darrel with video camera in hand called after Stephen. He laughed; he was in a relaxed mood. His arm went around my shoulder and he gave me a squeeze, then bent down to my level. I looked so short standing next to him. He grinned as he said,

'I remember when I stood next to Grandma – her head came under my armpit.'

This was a great day. His happiness was all we needed to relax and enjoy ourselves. He didn't stick with us; he wandered around on his own with his small green bag slung over his shoulder, enjoying the display of rockets, and recovered space junk and testing equipment.

When our 45 minutes were up, we straggled aboard and the driver did a head count. Someone was missing. One of the elderly ladies, who had taken a shine to Stephen, said in a slow Australian drawl, 'That nice young man who was sitting in front of me isn't here.'

Stephen was missing! Darrel and I were stunned, but we said nothing. What could we say? We hadn't seen him walk off. And everyone except Tom and Elaine thought he was a lone traveller.

My anxiety mounted and all I could think of was, 'Please, let's find him quickly.'

Joe the bus driver shook his head. As we drove slowly around Woomera, everyone was on the lookout for him. 'There he is!' someone shouted. Stephen was coming out of a shop with a drink in hand. What felt to us like an agonisingly long time had only been about five minutes. He stepped onto the bus, saying, 'I just went to get a drink. You said six o'clock. It's only one minute past,' and headed to a spare seat at the back of the bus. It was as if no one else existed. Or at least that's the way it appeared. But who knows what was going on in his mind? He was unpredictable already, at this early stage of the trip. We wondered what would happen next.

The next stop was Coober Pedy, famous for its opal mines and quality gems. The town sits amidst a stony, treeless desert. We passed a soccer field made completely of dirt; there were no lawns or grass to be seen anywhere in the township. This was our first overnight stay.

The sun streamed through our bedroom window, announcing a new day. It was time to move on. We struggled with our bags through the open door. Stephen came striding down the pathway, grabbed our bags and headed for the bus. He had just finished doing the same for Tom, Elaine and Alice.

'Here comes the man to carry all the bags down. Hey! I've got to get this on video!' Darrel grabbed the camera off the bed and focused it on Stephen, who gave an amused chuckle, and kept walking.

'Darrel, please be careful – he may not like you videoing him,' I whispered.

Stephen won the hearts of all the passengers because he was quiet and polite. To them, he was just a nice young man, and one of them joked that she wished he could marry her granddaughter.

With breakfast over and five minutes to go, we all headed for the bus. Stephen arrived to eat, as we were leaving the dining room. He had been busy carrying everyone's' cases to the bus.

'We leave in five minutes, Stephen,' the bus driver said gently, but sternly. 'I still have about three minutes to eat and I have a right to have breakfast. It is not eight o'clock yet' responded Stephen.

I heard the words, 'Stop nagging me!' in the tone of his voice. He gulped down coffee and toast and, when he came aboard, the driver made a comment about him being late. Stephen said nothing and joined Tom at the rear of the bus. Protective mother that I was, I thought: *Give him a break, he's only one minute late.*

Part of our tour of this underground town included visiting an opal mine, where we learnt how the opals were graded, cut and polished, and made into jewellery. We admired the pieces for sale; they were exquisite, but also expensive.

Stephen called me over to the display cabinet of pendants he was looking at. 'Which one would you like, Mum?'

An Awkward Fit

I was sure my heart was breaking – so much pain – so much joy. Having him be so kind and loving and yet being the reason for so much of my anxiety was almost too much to bear. I hugged him. I was happy again and I pointed to a pendant with a small but colourful stone. It was a pale blue with red and green lights shining through it.

He bought it and handed it to me. I was speechless. I knew he loved us as we adored him, but to show me in this manner really blew me away. With tears in my eyes, I hugged him again and, although it was difficult to find any words, I said, 'Stephen it's beautiful – to me it's priceless! This means more to me than you know.'

We stopped at the border, where people took the customary photos of each other with a foot in both South Australia and the Northern Territory. My eyes fixed on our son, a handsome figure with his hair falling around his shoulders and his head leaning slightly to one side, a can of beer in his hand. Joe the driver approached and chatted him about drinking on the bus. Joe had become edgy with this passenger who stood apart from the rest. He seemed to be waiting for him to do something wrong. I felt protective and resented the driver assuming Stephen intended to break the no-drinking-on-the-bus rule. One of Stephen's many good points was his respect for rules, and he would have had no intention of taking the beer on the bus. The moment passed without incident.

Stephen called out to Darrel, video camera at the ready, to film him walking across the border. It sounds crazy, but this small incident of Stephen relating to his father made me feel so good. As we boarded the bus, Joe the driver had noticed Darrel talking to Stephen. 'Who is he, anyway? He's on his own, he hasn't come with anyone. I'm trying to work him out,' the driver said.

'He's with us, he's our son,' Darrel replied. The driver obviously hadn't checked the surnames of his passengers.

As the third day got under way, I noticed Stephen was a little apart from the rest of the group, and not really interacting with anyone. Even I couldn't get more than a single word out of him.

He enjoyed looking at the sights and taking in the information, but he seemed like a tourist on his own. I felt uneasy but said nothing to Darrel, who kept focusing the camera on Stephen, making jokes and encouraging him to respond.

We were at Standley Chasm, 50 kilometres west of Alice Springs. It was like standing at the base of a mountain that had parted in the middle and looking up at two tall red walls reaching up to a bright blue sky. It was spectacular. Stephen was squatting on the ground, collecting soil samples. He did this at every place we visited, bagging and labelling them neatly. At an earlier stop, when Darrel videoed him collecting sand, Stephen had laughed and said, jokingly, 'I figured if I collect enough I could sell them when I get back to Adelaide.'

On the bus heading towards Alice Springs, I noticed Tom with his head down, absorbed in something. Every so often, he would look out the window and then back down. I peeped over his shoulder and saw he was sketching the scenery. A little while later, he would get out his watercolours and paint as we went along.

We arrived at Alice Springs with three hours to walk around and get some lunch. Everyone went their own way. Again, when it was time to leave, we had all assembled except for Stephen. Each time this happened, though, it wasn't necessarily because he was late. Often he was on time but, because the others were early, it didn't look good for him. I think the driver got annoyed because he would have liked to have taken off a little early, sometimes.

At the Royal Flying Doctor Service in Alice Springs, we watched a video on the work they do. It showed pictures of rescues at Uluru, where people had fallen from the rock. We were warned that if we weren't sure about our health or ability to climb the rock we should not attempt it.

We then drove up a hill to the scenic lookout. Stephen was sharing jokes with his dad. I guess most of the tourists didn't chat a lot. Anyway, we were too busy looking at the scenery and listening to the bus driver telling a bit of history about each place we went to.

Later, we headed for Ross River Homestead where we ate damper with a cup of tea before trying our hand at throwing boomerangs and cracking whips. As the youngest and tallest of our group, Stephen volunteered to retrieve the boomerangs that landed on the thatched roof of the arbour. When he had a go at whip cracking, the passengers encouraged him, saying, 'Go on, Stevie, have a go.'
He used to be able to handle a whip when he was at Roseworthy, but with lack of practice he wasn't up to his former standard and was a little embarrassed by that. We passed up the chance for a camel ride as Joe said we were stopping somewhere on the way back, where it would be cheaper.

Back on the bus again, many slept or dozed or generally retreated into their own private worlds. Darrel and I were at the front of the bus. I got out the video camera and walked down the aisle filming the scene. Stephen was watching me, occasionally bending his head looking for something. When I got close and aimed the video at him, he brought out his camera and snapped a picture of me videoing him. It warmed my heart to see the grin on his face and the sparkle in his eyes. The relief I felt when our son acted normally and actually showed a bit of humour was indescribable.
As Joe had promised, the camel farm on the return journey was cheaper and many people lined up for a ride. We weren't all as brave as we pretended but we didn't want to be outdone by the other passengers. Even 90-year-old Alice had a ride, perched behind her daughter.

Stephen disappeared. I couldn't see him anywhere. While we were on the camel, I kept thinking he would show up after we'd all finished and the camels had been put away, but thankfully that didn't happen. I heard one of the elderly women call, 'Come on, Stevie! Come for a camel ride.'

As always, he gave a polite smile in place of a verbal response, and yes, he did have a ride. Later, Tom told us he hadn't been feeling well and Stephen had gone back to the bus to check on him.

It was not long after this that Stephen was again last for the bus. The other passengers appreciated Stephen's politeness and help, and could see the driver was not impressed with him always being the last one to arrive. This particular morning, when it happened again, no one went aboard until Stephen arrived.

'We're not getting on the bus till Stevie comes,' chanted Marie 'He won't be the last one this time.' It was beautiful. I could have kissed the whole lot of them. And to think I was worried about Stephen fitting in with older passengers!

One of the highlights of the tour was our visit to Kata Tjuta and Uluru.

Kata Tjuta was our first stop and, from a distance, looked like Uluru, until we got closer. While Uluru is one single solid rock, Kata Tjuta is a series of large rocks. (*Uluru and Kata Tjuta were previously called Ayers Rock and The Olgas*).

I don't know how Marie got to know about Stephen's sore shoulder. Perhaps she noticed the times he put his hand on his neck to massage it or stretch his muscles. Anyway, when we arrived at the lookout to Kata Tjuta, Darrel had the video camera at work and found Stephen with his shirt off and Marie massaging his neck, while another woman was fanning him. They were most embarrassed at being caught on video!

Shortly after, as the bus headed along the track that led into Kata Tjuta, Stephen said he'd run out of film, so Darrel volunteered to take some photos for him. As Darrel and I walked together, looking at the amazing rock formations,

Stephen came hurtling up behind. I turned and was stunned to see the thunderous look on his face. He suddenly totally lost it, and he shouted at Darrel. 'You said you'd take photos for me, so why aren't you doing it? Go on! Take some – don't just stand there!'

Darrel was speechless. He turned and walked back to the bus, wounded. Stephen strode further up the path, the distance between us growing quickly.

What is going wrong? I don't believe Stephen said that – why is he like this?

I was shocked.

'Stephen, come back here! I want to talk to you!' I yelled.

Somehow I knew I could still exercise my position as his mother and he would listen. I was so angry with him.

'How could you talk to your father like that?' I shouted. 'You haven't even told him what photos you want him to take. That was not fair. You owe him an apology.'

Stephen stomped away without replying. I headed back to the bus .Any fight I had left was gone. I gave up, feeling totally defeated.

Not many of the passengers had walked to the lookout; it was too far for some of the older ones. Most had just gone for short walks not far from the bus and had witnessed the exchange between us.

The bus driver came up to Darrel. 'Go after him,' he said.

'No way – I'm not getting my head punched in!'

The bus driver went instead and returned walking alongside Stephen, with arms folded, quietly talking to him. However, one of the passengers who made it to the lookout later told us that, when Stephen arrived, he exploded and said a lot of angry things. At times, we were totally perplexed at what was happening to him. He kept losing his grip on reality and I felt that we were losing him to somewhere terrifying.

Our journey continued towards Uluru, and we stopped for lunch. I couldn't prevent the tears from flowing. I only wiped them off when they ran down my chin, so no one would realise I was so upset. I was inconsolable; there are no words to describe the fear and anxiety I felt.

The prospect of Stephen's future hung over me like a dark cloud. There were so many things I wanted to say to him but couldn't. *My grieving for him had begun*, but even then I didn't realise the full capabilities of this insidious psychological illness. I was so frightened for him. Some of the passengers noticed and tried to comfort me, which only made me worse.

By the time we returned to the bus, I had managed to stop the tears and bit my bottom lip to stop it from trembling, but I didn't feel any better. Darrel and I sat in separate seats. We had nothing to say, and we needed time to be by ourselves.

The incident was over for Stephen almost as quickly as it had begun. He sat beside me and said quietly, 'Are you alright, Mum?'

I just nodded. So much to say – no words to say them.

As I am writing this, tears are flowing. My need to tell this incident is so strong. To me, it's the only way I can put it in perspective and hopefully diminish some of the painful memories. I wish now that I wasn't so emotional and could have had a talk with Steve; there is so much I can think of that I should have said.

After about five minutes, he left me and sat next to his dad. Nothing was said about the verbal attack; there was just his presence, trying silently to console us. Stephen kept a notebook to record each sample of sand he collected, the date and the place. There was no record of sand for that day.

He simply wrote, 'No sand collected, no photographs taken at the Olgas.'

To Stephen, it was something that had happened and was now forgotten. He was relaxed and himself again. He chatted quietly to Tom, and smiled and said a few words when other passengers spoke to him.

Darrel and I started relaxing, and looked forward to the next stop. That afternoon we arrived at Uluru, where we would spend three hours. As most of the passengers were of the older generation, only three people decided to climb to the top: Morris, who looked to be in his mid fifties but very fit; Dawn, in her twenties; and Stephen. They set off, with the rest of us watching. It was an amazing sight; Stephen left the others behind and literally ran up the rock face. Darrel and I walked part way around the base of the rock, a large formation that looked like a prehistoric animal crouching in the desert.

After Stephen headed off, the driver approached Darrel and asked if he'd have a word with our son about always turning up late.

'I'm not doing it. You handle it yourself,' said Darrel. He didn't want another outburst from Stephen.

On a later occasion, the driver said to Darrel, 'I think I've worked him out.'

Darrel replied, 'No, you haven't, mate. He has real problems,' and proceeded to tell just a little of what Stephen was going through. From then on, Joe was more understanding. He also had difficulties he was going through with his own family.

Stephen stood on top of the rock with the video camera and made a documentary for us on what he could see. It was very well done. He had absorbed much of the information Joe had given us and also had read up on it. He sounded like his dad, who is also very knowledgeable about Australian history and geography.

Small things were important to Stephen, such as taking the video camera on to the Rock so we would know exactly what he saw. Similarly, collecting soil from every place we visited and keeping a written record was vital to him. Knowing this, I volunteered to collect a soil sample from the rock base.

As our departure time drew near, we all waited anxiously to catch sight of the climbers. Luckily, we had binoculars; otherwise we would not have known who they were. First, we saw Morris, then Dawn. With anxious hearts, Darrel and I waited about another ten minutes for Stephen to come into view. It looked like he would be last on the bus again. About halfway down, he started running. The hair on the back of my neck stood up .The downward path was a ridge with terrifying drops on both sides. He could easily have lost his footing. He passed Dawn and Morris and reached the bottom within minutes.

Dawn was in trouble; she froze, she was full of fear and could go no further. Everyone held their breath, as they waited to see what would happen next. The moment Stephen realised she wasn't going to make it by herself, he ran back up as fast as he'd come down. His emotional difficulties and hyperactivity sometimes worked to others' advantage, and he could sense danger. Gently, he helped her down, and everyone cheered as they approached the bus. Morris came down a few minutes later.

From there, the bus headed to the lookout so we could view the rock at sunset. As we gathered to watch, Stephen sat next to his father as if nothing had happened between them. He was happy and relaxed as he ate the cold chicken pack provided for dinner. We sat watching the sun set over the rock. Some of us sat on the kerb; others stood transfixed by this majestic monstrosity. It was changing colour in front of us. Over a half hour period, the rock changed from bright orange to light brown, then dark brown to purple. It was a spectacular sight. Tears of pain and pleasure trickled down my cheeks. I wiped them with the flat of my hand. No one saw them; no one was supposed to see them.

Our trip home was not without incident. As we pulled into the roadhouse at Glendambo for lunch and fuel, we knew from the strange noise the bus was making that something was not right. It was the exhaust, a major problem that meant waiting for a mechanic to come and fix it. Part of the exhaust had come off and it sounded like an old tractor chugging along the road. During our five-hour wait, we investigated every nook and cranny of this small settlement. We bought food, with some passengers washing it down with a beer or two from the only pub in town, and the pinball machine got a thorough workout. We must have bought nearly all the souvenirs in town, too, just to have something to do. I bought Stephen a tank top as a reminder of our trip. The mechanic arrived after about three hours but, because we couldn't get the broken part replaced in time for us to be back in Adelaide that evening, it was decided to patch it up as best we could and keep going.

From the Adelaide bus depot, we were taken home by van. The three of us were in good spirits and glad to be back. When we got home, however, we discovered no one had a house key, and the place was as secure as Fort Knox.
'Let's throw a brick at the smallest window,' I suggested. This was to no avail as the brick kept bouncing off, which meant there was no choice but to go for a larger window. So we did, and Stephen climbed in and opened the door. We could all see the funny side of the situation and had a good laugh at our stupidity. It was a great wind-down to what had been in many ways a nerve-racking trip. Yet, despite everything, it was time well spent together. I felt lucky to have Stephen with us. No matter how much stress was in our lives, he was ultimately supportive and helpful, he could not help what was happening to him and he received no pleasure from upsetting us.

It was late, so Stephen stayed the night. At about seven the next morning, I walked out the back door and nearly died of fright, for on the lawn I saw what looked like a white goanna. It was huge, and staring straight at me. I screamed, before realising it was a garden decoration. It certainly had not been there the night before. At my scream, Stephen came running, and laughed when he realised what had happened. As usual, unable to sleep he had been wandering around the house at about 2 am when he heard a noise out the front and went to investigate. Driving around the street was a car with a trailer full of garden ornaments, and two young men giving each household a gnome or similar decoration.

'What's this? Did you flog them?' Stephen asked. 'No,' they said. It was a promotion and they were giving them away. 'Pick the one you want,' they said, and that's how I ended up with the goanna, the biggest ornament on the trailer. I love it, because it holds special meaning; I would never part with it. We didn't hear any more about that strange Robin Hood act that took place in the early hours of the morning. There were certainly a lot of bewildered neighbours that day.

Tom, Elaine and Alice were due to fly home to England in two days' time and were booked into the West Beach Caravan Park for their final two nights. They hadn't been to Adelaide before and Stephen wanted to show them around. He wanted to take them up to Mount Lofty to see the magical fairyland view that the lights of Adelaide offered, and he asked if they could spend the night with us. Of course, I said, it would be a pleasure to have them.

Stephen spent that evening and the next day as tour guide for his friends. He took them on the ride of a lifetime to see all the sights of Adelaide he could cram into an afternoon. When they said their good-byes they invited him to visit them in England. He assured them he would be there in about two years, and he would be at the airport next morning at five o'clock to say goodbye. Stephen tore into the airport the next morning, just as the plane for England was taking off. Tom and Elaine never saw him again.

CHAPTER 21 – 1997 - A place to call home

What makes me tick?
What makes me me?
Sick people can be very strong!

One day, reality will be a place for ghosts and only survival will limit mankind. I am stunned by my own complexities, but embarrassed at my inability to decipher which is relevant or correct. And my inability to concentrate on one point at a time without forgetting the others or getting confused trying to remember them all. Only a loony would bother to write this.

~

On returning home from our bus tour to central Australia, I continued helping Stephen find somewhere to live. He needed somewhere he could feel comfortable and secure and, most importantly, a place he could continue working on his car.

Over the past 12 months, Stephen and I had been negotiating with the Housing Trust for him to obtain priority housing. He was paranoid about living with neighbours who could see over his fence, or even the possibility of them being in their front garden where he would come in contact with them when he left his house. He was looking for somewhere quiet and secluded. Since living in his flat in Ponton Street Salisbury in 1994, Stephen had not settled and had kept moving from place to place.

The Housing Trust initially refused his application because they felt he did not qualify for priority housing. Stephen needed to provide more information for them to review his situation. He talked to our local Member of Parliament who negotiated with the Housing Trust, and he also obtained a letter from Graham, his psychologist, supporting his claim that he was in urgent need of suitable accommodation because of his medical condition.

In the middle of October 1997, a housing unit became available in Gawler West, which was offered to Stephen. The two-bedroom unit, set in a small courtyard, was almost new and absolutely perfect, with only one unit visible from his front garden, belonging to an elderly lady who lived alone. The adjoining unit was set back a little, hidden by bushes, and was home to a young man about Stephen's age with cerebral palsy who was difficult to understand when he spoke.

Stephen was clearly very excited about moving into his new home and started making plans. He would build an enclosure for his car; he had already spoken to his new neighbours and they had no problems with his working on the car and making noise, within reason. The rent was also good. He would have reduced rent because he was unemployed. Darrel told him it was about time he had a decent break and things started working out for him. Stephen nodded in agreement.

He was in the midst of making plans to move in when he received a devastating telephone call from Andrew, who was handling the application for priority housing. Andrew had made an error. He had not taken into account that Stephen had been awarded one-year's salary by WorkCover, which meant he would have to pay the full rent. This was much more than Stephen could afford, if his money was going to last until November.

'What? No bloody way! You can't do this! What mistake? You don't make mistakes like that!' Stephen exploded down the phone at the man on the other end, who kept apologising profusely and trying to explain the situation through Stephen's roaring.

I grabbed the phone from Stephen and he started walking around and around the room, shouting, 'He can't do that to me! That's not right! If you say it's one thing, then you don't change your mind.'

It was happening again, the sudden loss of control. This was the second time I had seen him so upset – I was really scared for him. How could this quiet, gentle person suddenly become so out of control? We didn't know how this problem was going to sort itself out. It was as though we were all being sucked into a vortex, struggling to escape.

We didn't realise that this invasive psychotic behaviour, this sudden personality change and verbal aggression, was never going to fix itself. We didn't understand the condition or the full implication of what schizophrenia was; we knew of no information or support groups. We were ignorant of the implications of the dangers of suicide or self-harm; deep down, we were hoping things would sort themselves out.

Andrew, on the other end of the phone, apologised to me again and explained what had happened. I was more interested in making him realise the situation he had created by his mistake.

It was too late for apologies. If we had known the rent was going to be so high, we would have refused it without looking at the unit. It was a bad mistake to make to someone who has schizophrenia. Stephen had his heart set on it. He would now take it, even though there was no way he could find the money to pay for it.

In his mind, Stephen was already restoring his car in the shed he had built; the small secluded backyard with its high fences already had his small garden shed in the far corner; and he had paved the yard area and pruned the apricot and peach trees. The garden plans had already been drawn up and the seeds had been planted; the snapdragons were already in flower along the border. At last, his life had come together and he was at peace.

They couldn't take it away from him. I tried to make him understand he could not afford the rent but he couldn't see it – he would find a way. He was not going to let them rob him of his goal. He paid $4000 in advance. This was the last of his money.

On 1 November 1997, his mate, Chris helped him move. The unit was not far from where Stephen's friend Linda and her daughter were living. Stephen was happy and became absorbed in setting up his new home. He asked my advice on curtain colours for the lounge room; we bought him a lounge suite and he colour-coordinated the rooms. He bought new towels, bath mats and hand towels, all in green. He worked tirelessly in the garden for several days and it began to take shape. Once he moved in, he seemed to settle down. We all relaxed.

It was Christmas, 1997. Stephen joined us around the Christmas tree. He was in good spirits and arrived with a gift for everyone. We exchanged presents. Our grandson Ryan, 18 months old, was caught up in the excitement of tearing paper off the presents to find fun things inside.
'Look at this!' Nicole had taken the lid off a tin of biscuits and held them out for Ryan to take one. 'Watch! He gets so excited, he can't choose.'
Ryan was sitting on the floor reaching for a biscuit but he couldn't take one – he was too excited to choose. His little hand was shaking and his tiny face was animated. Stephen sternly interrupted. 'Don't make him do that. Give him a biscuit! There's too many for him to choose from.'
Stephen chose a biscuit and handed it to Ryan. The muscles in the back of my neck tensed. I could see that he was identifying with his nephew. He was recognising the same complexities and confusion that he had experienced frequently in his own life.

An Awkward Fit

Darrel had chosen the perfect gift for our son .A Coopers home-brew beer kit.

Our phone rang the day after Christmas. It was Graham, Stephen's psychologist. 'Stephen left a Christmas greeting on my answering machine and I am returning his call. How is he going? I haven't heard from him for some months.'

'He's doing well,' I told him. 'He's living in Gawler and seems quite happy.'

Helen Maczkowiack

CHAPTER 22 – 1998 - Beer for two

This Christmas my dad gave me a Coopers Micro-brew kit. Just the very nature of the gift meant a great deal to me, let alone the fun I'd have putting it together, following each step ever so carefully, and the enjoyment of sharing my first homebrew with my dad.

I gladly accepted Dad's offer to help for I knew his experience with home brewing over many years might ensure a great-tasting beer. I became pleased and excited when the bubbles of escaping gas told of a healthy fermentation process in action.

Four days later the bubbles slowed and on day five all was silent. Day six and it's time to bottle.

When labelling, I started from bottle no. 28 so that it would be first in the cupboard and last to drink. I guess that way the last bottle coming from the bottom of the brew might just have that little longer to settle. The problem with this idea is that by the time I worked my way down the bottles I had run out of labels. I was thrilled to discover they had come as a bonus pack with CSR/Coopers carbon stickers.

As you would guess, I can do nothing less than offer my dad a beer from the first bottle. Unlike the last bottles, they have proper Cooper's labels, which I proudly wrote in the brewed-by section 'Father and Son' and the brewing date 26-12-97 – 2-1-98.

~

Our Christmas present to Stephen was the gift of all gifts. We couldn't have chosen better. After the first successful batch, he decided that if he doubled the sugar it would increase the alcohol content and would be pretty deadly.

His mates thought it was okay, too, and offered to pay him to make some for them.

Stephen thought it could be quite a lucrative business. The only thing he forgot was that he wasn't home when it was ready to be bottled and Darrel and I ended up in his Gawler flat bottling a very potent batch of beer until 1.00 am on a Sunday morning. And thoroughly enjoying the whole experience of being surrounded by empty beer bottles waiting their turn to be filled. We laughed about finding ourselves in this ridiculous situation, and feeling very much like we had been conned by our son.

It was amazing; Stephen seemed so different, so calm and all together. But it didn't turn out to be that simple; his illness surfaced when we least expected. We were on a roller-coaster ride. Small things would set him off, and we were walking on broken glass.

Stephen's money was gone. There was no income except for odd jobs I was finding around our house for him to do, and Chris's dad, who lived on a hobby farm while working as a teacher, had him stay for a week to do some welding and set up programs on the school computers. Stephen raided my food cupboard so that he could contribute something towards the cost of his stay at the farm.

He continued drawing from his two bank accounts until the banks started demanding their money back. Stephen couldn't accept that because they had his money in the bank for months they couldn't carry him financially until he was able to obtain an income and pay them back. He became very depressed and anxious about his financial position. He also owed money for electricity and the phone. He kept getting letters from the bank and his credit union demanding that he pay back the money or incur a hefty interest bill.

I took over his financial affairs. Stephen signed a letter I wrote to the banks explaining his financial and medical situation, followed by a phone call from me pleading with them to understand and come to a manageable agreement so we could pay back the several thousand dollars he now owed.

'I'm going to Barmera with Wolly to find work,' announced Stephen, standing on the front porch of our house. Wolly was the nickname of his friend, who was also called William. Wolly had a job with an irrigation firm in the Riverland and Stephen hoped to get work there, too. Within a week, he had found employment and the boys were renting a small holiday unit overlooking beautiful Lake Bonney in Barmera at a cost of $90 a week. He wouldn't give up the Gawler unit and there was not much of the $4,000 left that he had paid in advance.

CHAPTER 23 – 1998 - A nonsensical situation

I had suffered two days without sleep, so I went to a doctor who prescribed Valium (diazepam), to settle me down. I ingested 20 mg at 4 pm in the main street of Gawler. It takes ten minutes to get home. Thirty minutes after taking the tablets, I was finally able to sleep. I slept for five hours (not much, considering the length of time since I last slept – five hours Sunday morning).

I woke suddenly at 9.30 pm with startling speed, jumping out of bed and feeling like a tightly wound spring.

At 1.30 am on Wednesday, while pacing up and down to relieve my restlessness, I suddenly felt this shifting sensation in my thoughts and presence of mind ... lasting for about 30 seconds. [It] seemed that my thought processing pathways had pulled themselves into alignment, causing me to feel well balanced, clear-headed and perfectly at ease in dealing with whatever situation and thoughts were at hand. Many of the things that I have studied and huge pieces of my life, which I generally have trouble remembering, came to me with ease. The feeling of constant torment lifted like a great weight and I became ... much to my relief, an emotionally sound human being.

I experienced the exact same thing before Christmas. I had a wisdom tooth pulled which had become severely infected, and made an appointment to go see a GP in Craigmore. I was prescribed the usual antibiotics as well as morphine tablets for the chronic pain I was in. I had never received [it] before, and everyone I've ever heard speak about the drug told what they had experienced.

As to last night, as soon as the sensation passed, the full impact of the extent to which I am troubled by my affliction and how it has interfered with my interaction with others and destroyed my prospects of reaching my full potential hit home. I lapsed into total emotional breakdown. After some time, I forced myself to think of things, places and funny events to curb my depression. It would have been funny to watch as I laughed and cried at the same time. I felt a great need to talk to someone, but not only was everyone I knew asleep, but it would be a pointless exercise, resulting in my friends eventually getting sick of me. Although talking with certain people sometimes calms me down, I knew that talking could not make me feel NORMAL, or make the disease go away.

Most people end up telling me my problems are all in my head (as if I didn't already know), and that I should deal with them like everyone else, or ignore it and get on with my life – how blind, annoying and frustrating they are. Those people just don't get it! They end up treating me with contempt and eventually give me the cold shoulder. Getting on with my life is easy ... coping with it isn't.

4.40 am on reflection:
One could argue what it is to be normal, e.g. it's normal that there exists in the world people that are noticeably different and that if they weren't, then they wouldn't be who they are. Maybe it's my make-up that I am who I am. That who I am now with the problems that I seem to have may be considered normal behaviour and normal psychological responses, given my life's experience (environment).

Should my lot in life [have] been different or the world I live in, I may still be susceptible to becoming what I am now, but seem to be a completely different person both in my mind and in the eyes of others and never experience the torment that I live with now ... hmm, I didn't explain this too well.

It's just that all the doctors tell me and I read about treatments that allow people [to] live without the torment, yet they refuse to try/prescribe anything that generally helps, that is, I'm a full-on insomniac who sleeps when I'm either physically or mentally exhausted (nothing to do with my sleeping schedule) ... who made the rules as to when a person should sleep? I'm a night-shift worker. If the medication that helps people sleep is refused to someone like me, then who the bloody hell are they meant for? What's the point of even having them? They say that the drugs that would allow me to be normal ... not euphoric or doped out (I couldn't call that normal) are too strong and it's too easy to become dependent. Even should that happen as a result of bad management, how can they expect me to give a shit! ... at least addiction can be treated ... it's got to be better than this ... hmm.

It occurred to me while writing this out by hand that you may be interested in reading this. I feel foolish to some degree for writing this, as some would consider this sort of thinking or such an exercise to be stupid and a waste of time. Others would say it shows me to be a deep thinker with interesting insights. Taking a step back ... maybe I'd make a good lab guinea pig – ha ha ha.
I guess I wouldn't bother with it if I were sure either way. If I knew whether my feelings of genuine insight, while at the same time my feeling of self-delusion, were valid ... I feel inadequate to make this determination. I apologise ... don't mean to dump on you!

~

Stephen worked five days a week, installing irrigation systems on properties, and worked most of his weekends picking fruit to finance both rents and his debts. He would come home from work like a tightly wound spring and then spend all night unwinding, to get ready to face work the next day.

I tried to explain to him that what he was trying to accomplish was near impossible. Even though he was working, he could not afford to pay rent on both places, buy food and keep a car on the road. Perhaps he should stay in Barmera and give up his flat? He couldn't. The Gawler unit represented his dream for the future. His mind was set in one direction, living in Gawler, restoring his car and living close to his family and friends.

Every third weekend, Stephen came home to Gawler. Often on Sunday he and his work mate Wolly would come to us for dinner. I would cook a roast and they would take home what was left over. Stephen barely sat still long enough to eat before he'd be up moving around the room, talking all the while and looking anxious and tired. We were aware he was still under incredible pressure; we could see it in his movements. He never left our house without giving us both a hug and saying, 'I love you.' Darrel filled his car with fuel for his journey back to Barmera and his work.

It would not be long before the money he had paid for the rent on the Gawler West unit would run out and he would have to find more money. He was already working every day of the week and most of his earnings went into paying off the bank debts.

I made an appointment with CentreLink, an agency that delivers a range of services to the community, including unemployment benefits and pensions. I wanted to see if there was some way that he could get an invalid pension, because of his illness, so that he could come back to live in Gawler. How much longer could he keep up this pace?

I was taken into a small cubicle, where I sat opposite a very sympathetic woman about my own age. I began explaining the situation. She suggested that he find a job closer to home, but he was unable to do this. He was desperate to work as many hours as possible to get more money. She offered a few more suggestions while I tried to explain all the reasons they wouldn't work. I ended up getting nowhere because I was crying too much for her to understand what I was saying. I was so embarrassed at my lack of control over my emotions. The agony of trying to explain a nonsensical situation left me speechless.

Stephen was home for the weekend of my nephew's eighteenth birthday party in June, 1998. As we walked into the Morphett Vale clubrooms, I saw the smiling faces of my extended family. We didn't get to see them very often because they lived south of Adelaide and we lived in the north, 90 minutes away. I come from a large family of three brothers and four sisters. Most of them were at the party and it was good to catch up.

I felt Stephen's apprehension. He had already spoken about his concern regarding his uncle under whom he had worked when he injured himself at the foundry. They had not had an opportunity to talk about it since then, and Stephen felt his uncle had let him down. I didn't want to take Stephen's feelings upon myself, but it always happened this way; I just knew how he felt without even asking him.

After a few whiskies, Stephen loosened up and talked to Jeff, my sister Cheryl's husband, about what happened at the engineering firm, and felt a lot better. Stephen didn't stray far from my side, which did concern me because this meant he was feeling insecure even with his relatives. The party ran out of beer and Darrel took Stephen with him to the bottle shop to buy more. Darrel was obviously very concerned about Stephen's state of mind and told him, 'Don't ever think about taking your life. Don't ever make your mother go through that.'

'No,' he said. 'I wouldn't.'

The following day, Nicky, her husband Murray and their two children went to the park with Stephen for a picnic lunch. Nicky thought it was about time Stephen spent some time with his nephews, and took photos using his camera. Stephen spent most of his time with his godson Ryan on the play equipment, and then kicked a ball to him. He underestimated the limited strength of the toddler and poor Ryan's legs were whisked from under him as the ball ploughed through. He wasn't hurt, but became quite upset. That same evening Stephen returned to his job in Barmera.

The horticultural course he did at Roseworthy College, and his experience working on fruit orchards, made Stephen's job installing irrigation systems very easy for him.

From my perspective, things appeared to settle down a little for him in the next few weeks. On visits home, he was happy to talk about his work and some of its interesting aspects. He was fast, reliable and efficient, and the boss gave him a pay rise.

'My boss has asked if I am interested in making a career out of this type of work, but I said no.'

'Why?' I asked. 'This is a good opportunity for you. It's the sort of thing you have been trained for, and you love working outside.' I thought this was the answer to our prayers; he had the opportunity to make things work for him.

'No. It's too lonely being up there by myself. I miss my friends.'

I checked the employment section of the paper each day, hoping to find a suitable job so he could come home. Stephen would keep 50 dollars for himself and give me the rest of his wages to pay off the debts that were a constant source of stress for him. The money he handed over was enough to slowly reduce the debt, but there was nothing left over for him to save. So we began looking for someone to rent the Gawler unit while he was away working.

Bill, the son of a friend of ours, agreed to take over the unit and, before he moved in, I gave it a thorough cleaning. Among several pot plants out the back, I found a seedling that looked like marijuana. I was quite concerned because Bill was the son of a chief inspector of police. The following weekend, when Stephen came home, I asked him about it. He said he had no idea what plant it was – they often appeared in his pot plants, but it definitely wasn't marijuana. I hate to say it, but that didn't convince me at all. I had a vivid recollection of the small plant he had me look after while he was in Roseworthy College. I couldn't bring myself to destroy the plant, so I hid it behind the garden shed.

Bill lasted three weeks renting the Gawler unit, and then decided that it was too lonely living by himself, and moved out. Everything was calm, uneventful. It was as if the craziness had stopped. Or had it? Was I just being left alone to take a breather before a storm? I could feel it building up in me. How was Stephen feeling? Was this also what he was experiencing?

While still working at the kindergarten, my mind was constantly on Stephen, trying to remove some of the obstacles in his life and create hope for the future. I rang the Housing Trust to ask if he could erect the shed at the Gawler unit he so badly wanted, so that, when he moved back to Gawler, he could continue restoring his car. I remember thinking it's a good thing I only work part-time or I'd have to give up work for a while so I could cope with the pressures that I felt were upon me.

In one of Stephen's Monday phone calls to Chris, his friend gave him the news I was dreading. 'You will have to get your car out of our car-port. We're moving in two weeks.'

Afraid of causing Stephen more anxiety and risking him feeling as if they were betraying him, they had decided that the nicest way of getting him to shift his car was to move house.

This did not prove too difficult a problem for Stephen. He handled it very well and, within a short time, announced that Linda would let him store it in her shed at Gawler. The next time he came home from Barmera, he spent the entire weekend shifting the cars from Chris's garage and my mother's shed to Linda's shed in Gawler. He knew this would only be a short-term solution, as she was also expecting to move house very shortly.

Stephen had problems with a second wisdom tooth. This one proved too difficult to be extracted by the dentist because of the position of the roots, and needed to be removed surgically. He made an appointment with the dental surgeon for a Friday afternoon.

It was now early July, 1998. Stephen stopped working at lunch time and drove the three hours home to Craigmore, and I drove him into the city for his appointment with the dental surgeon. All new patients were required to fill out an information form. He sat beside me and, when he came to the question, 'Do you suffer from depression/anxiety or any other psychological condition?' asked what he should write.

'Anxiety,' I suggested, with which he was quite comfortable.

On Saturday morning, Darrel and I drove Stephen to the hospital for day surgery to have the tooth removed. We drove past the zoo, where there had been an accident.

'Stop!' yelled Stephen, and was almost out the car before we had pulled into the kerb. He ran over to where an elderly man was sitting, half out of his car, holding his eye. Stephen's appointment was forgotten for the moment as he grabbed my phone from my bag, dialled for an ambulance and consoled the man while they waited for it to arrive.

'I told him he was okay and his eye wasn't too bad,' said Stephen when he got back in the car. 'But you should have seen it. It was ripped out and hanging on his cheek.'

We left Stephen at the hospital and were told to come back for him later that afternoon. I wouldn't go back with Darrel. I was afraid – the trauma we'd suffered on the drive home after his last wisdom tooth was removed was more than I could cope with again.

Stephen was semi-conscious and slowly coming around when Darrel went to collect him. He brought him home, but Stephen wanted to go back to his own unit. I made up a bottle of boiled salt water to use as a mouth rinse, and this time he accepted it without insisting it come from the chemist. *At least he wasn't paranoid about it being impure. I felt a surge of hope. Was he getting better?*
Stephen asked Darrel to take him to Linda's. He and Linda were spending a lot of the time together when Stephen was home from his work in Barmera.

A week after the operation, the receptionist at the dental surgery telephoned me twice to enquire about Stephen and gave me instructions on how to keep the gum from becoming infected. Why were they doing this? I wondered, although it was very kind of them. Stephen was off work for the next week or possibly two. He spent most of that time at Linda's.
Their relationship had developed into something very special. They had come to rely on each other for companionship.
Unlike last time, Stephen's gum was healing well and he was almost ready to resume his job in Barmera when Linda received news of the house she had been waiting for. She was moving within a week.
Those damn cars again!

Miracles don't happen all that often but we needed one now! I felt haunted by the need to help, each time Stephen needed somewhere to put his collection of EJ Holden cars. I couldn't handle seeing him so upset and anxious when he was backed into a corner, and this time he had run out of friends with garages.

How many people had a spare garage? We had already exhausted three locations. But I took the view that if you don't ask you don't get, and we were desperate. His plans for building an enclosure on the Gawler unit couldn't go ahead for another few months, until he'd finished the job at Barmera and was back living in the unit.

After three days of tossing around ideas, I came up with a possibility – a friend named Sue.

Sue was the speech pathologist assigned to the kindergarten where I worked. We were distantly related through Darrel's and her grandparents, and we had become good friends over the years. Because I often visited her parents on their farm in Gawler, I knew of a shed, a short distance from the family home, that had been erected by the fire department for storage, but was no longer in use. I was ready to beg for help, and they knew a little of Stephen's difficulties and he had done some paving work for Sue's grandmother some months earlier. With his promise that it would be no longer than three months, Stephen took over the shed with his accumulated car parts from at least three EJ Holdens. These included doors in various colours, several radiators hanging from the rafters, and many tyres, fan belts and radiator hoses. Everything was packed neatly and tightly together and covered with plastic sheets. The long-term intention was to relocate it all to Stephen's unit at Gawler, when he eventually built his shed. *I could see this heading for disaster again – no money, no shed.*

Stephen returned to his job in Barmera and came home three weeks later. Linda had been in her new house for a week. It was Saturday, 8 August, the day before Darrel's birthday, so Stephen brought Linda and the baby along to the Kingsford Hotel in Gawler for a celebration dinner.

Stephen was in good spirits and the perfect host. He helped Linda with Kailah, looking every bit the family man, and fussed over the baby as if she were his own. Linda had often remarked on how, when they went out together, people thought they were a family, and how much Kailah resembled them both. We talked about his job at Barmera, his house, the new floor covering we had recently put in our dining room and Linda's new house. After dinner, Linda invited us around for coffee .We hadn't been there before.

Darrel and I sat on the two single chairs watching the Crows' AFL match on TV. Stephen sprawled across the floor, playing with the new addition to the family, a tiny kitten. He was leaning against the lounge, the long legs of his 6ft 4in frame reaching halfway across the small lounge room. The kitten crawled around his neck and shoulders and got tangled in his long hair. He was completely relaxed as he enjoyed the kitten's antics, giving no indication of having any psychological problems. This was the Stephen that Linda knew. It was also the Stephen I wanted our son to be, and it had been so long since I had witnessed him like this. Throughout all his difficulties, Linda was the only close friend who knew nothing about the trauma he was going through. She accepted him unconditionally, and liked what he offered as a friend.

When they stayed overnight at each other's places and he kept her awake playing computer games or wanting to chat, she didn't judge him or think him mad. She just told him, 'Bugger off! I want to sleep,' and that was that. Linda tells it how she sees it; she is straightforward and honest, and I didn't fully appreciate what a great friendship they had until I wrote this book.

I remember Linda asking me once how I would feel if eventually they married. I don't remember my reply, but I never forgot her asking me.

CHAPTER 24 – 1998 - Sunset on the lake

If people do stupid things that can be avoided with a little thought, of course I'm going to get upset. I've put up with this kind of crap my whole life and won't any more!
It's about time others started being honest with themselves and showed me the same respect that they demand for themselves. It's the same everywhere I go. I'm sick of all the games and unnecessary bullshit. Everyone can take it and shove it. Wolly, thanks a fucking lot!
I don't care what you do but you could at least show me the courtesy of letting me know what's going on, instead of just vanishing! If I can show you this much respect, well by fuck so can you. Taking the house key was clever. If I'm home, what do you need it for!

Obviously you have intended to piss me off. Now you'll have to live with it! You only get back what you dish out. Be honest and trustworthy and be nice and that's what you'll get back! I don't like upsetting people. I wish I could get upset without upsetting other people too.
I'm careful because so many have pretended yet don't really intend to do the right thing.
I'm on my own. Wolly's gone to live with his aunty – he just up and left.

~

Stephen's flatmate Wolly, was no longer sharing the rent at Barmera, because he had become increasingly afraid of Stephen, who constantly paced the floor and often lost control of his emotions.Stephen had tried to get the land agent to reduce the rent because he couldn't afford to pay $90 on his own, but he was not successful.

It was Sunday. Stephen had been home for the weekend and was preparing to return to his job in Barmera. He sat on the shoebox in our laundry, pulling on his work boots. 'Only a few more weeks and I will be home again,' he said.

It was not hard to see how anxious he was to come back and resume the life he had left behind. He was only in Barmera for one reason and that was to pay off the money he owed the banks.

'A little more than a few weeks – it's not until November,' I told him.

Even over a little thing like this, I dreaded not being able to agree with him (he thought his job ended in September and it was now July), and I could see his spirit drain away and his shoulders droop.

'Look at me! I'm nearly 30 and I don't even have a decent job. You've always found my jobs for me, Mum. I'm afraid to even go for one because, even though I might be able to do the work, I always think there is someone else that could do it a lot better than I could. I don't seem to be getting anywhere; and I don't feel like I deserve a decent job, anyway.'

It seemed to him that everything was rotten in his life. Every path he went down smelt of mould and decay. This negativity was hard to get used to. As a child, Stephen had been so positive and full of confidence. If something didn't work out, he would move on to another project. He always had a positive outlook and mind-set. I put my arms around him.

'You've been through a lot, Stephen, give yourself a little more time, wait a little longer and things will turn out. You found this job in Barmera yourself and you are working hard.'

I made some other bland statement of reassurance and added a few more floundering sentences that didn't make a lot of sense, as he headed for the front door and back to his job at Barmera.

I followed him out to his car. 'I love you. Please be careful on the road.'

'Don't worry! I will.'

I felt defeated, ashamed, and devoid of any answers or solutions to give him. I was trying to find some words of hope to help his totally shattered ego – but I had none. He was suffering from shame at not being able to manage his own life. There and then, Darrel and I decided it was time to visit him in Barmera. We made arrangements to see him the following weekend.

This was our first visit since Stephen had started working in the Riverland. He rang on the Friday to check we were still coming; he was really looking forward to our visit.

'I'll meet you at the cabin, and then how about you come and help me pick mandarins?' he asked, giving us the address.

'Okay! We will buy lunch on the way there.'

'Great! Can you ask Linda if she'd like to come up and stay for a week?

She can come up with you. 'We phoned Linda and asked, but she was still settling into her new house. She had arranged for an electrician to come on the Saturday and said she'd go another time.

When we reached Barmera, we stopped at a shop and bought pies and pasties for lunch, then drove down to the lake looking for the address that Stephen had given us.

The line of featureless, small white cabins stood a little back from the dirt track that ran parallel to Lake Bonney in Barmera. We soon found the one Stephen was renting; his green station wagon stood in the driveway. There was a single entrance to each cabin from the left-hand side and there were windows at the back and front. The unit was square with a flat roof. It reminded me of the white limestone sulphur boxes we used for drying apricots during the fruit harvest on my father's property at Loxton, years ago.

Stephen greeted us. 'G'day! Didn't Linda come with you?'

As we entered, my eyes zeroed in on the exposed wooden beams of the ceiling. I felt uneasy, but my relief that Stephen looked so well over-rode that concern. The front room of the unit was a combined lounge/kitchen with only the barest of essentials. There was a sink, a stove and a noisy fridge in the kitchen, and the lounge had only one cushion, one tattered old armchair and a coffee table. It was typical worker's accommodation.

Hanging from the rafters was a fluorescent light that didn't work. Stephen had strung a cord from the light switch around the curtain rod, and this had a globe attached that also wasn't working. He managed by using a candle at night. There was no radio or TV and we noticed Stephen hadn't brought his guitar with him. In his spare time, he cleaned and polished the several car accessories and chrome parts he had brought from Gawler.

'What do you do after work? There's nothing here! Don't you have a radio?' asked Darrel, concern showing on his face.

'I'm usually too tired to do anything but sleep,' Stephen replied.

After lunch, we followed Stephen in our car as he wove along dirt roads and sandy tracks, past vineyards and orange groves. Fifteen minutes later, we reached the mandarin trees where we were to spend the afternoon picking fruit with him. He left his car door open so we could work to the music from his radio, and tried to show me how to use the snips so no stalk was left on the fruit.

I smiled, 'I've been using snips since before you were born! I grew up with fruit trees.'

'Oops! Sorry, Mum!' he grinned at me.

For some of the time, Stephen was on the cherry picker, reaching the fruit at the top of the trees; he worked hard and fast. At other times, he picked fruit alongside Darrel. They told jokes and chatted happily, like a father and son should when they're enjoying each other's company.

I started picking on the same tree as Stephen. He joked, 'That'd be right! Pinch all the big fruit! 'Then he added, 'Just imagine, Mum, if this was my fruit we were picking.'

'It could be, Steve,' I said soberly. 'You can own a property like this.' The subject was dropped and we went on picking.

After work, I inspected the shack before we left for the local hotel for dinner. Two small bedrooms branched off from the main room, one with an untidy double bed, and the remnants of what was once a built-in robe.

The other room was completely bare except for an old single bed turned on its side. There was no mattress. The old worn-out tiles were falling off the walls in the bathroom, there was no shower curtain, no cupboard, and the whole place was in desperate need of repair.

As Darrel took his turn in the shower, Stephen and I squatted next to each other against the wall of his unit and watched the beautiful warm colours of the sunset spread across the sky and reflect through the water of the lake .We sat together in silence for a moment, while the trees and grass around us moved gently in the breeze. The sun's rays lit up the clouds from underneath, turning them into a fiery red. The moment was magic.

'You know, Mum,' he said, 'with this view of the lake and the sunset, I'm amazed these units haven't been upgraded to make this into a real tourist resort. It has great potential. I wonder how much it would cost me to buy this unit and restore it? I could rent it out. Who else do you know lucky enough to come home from work each day and see this beautiful view of a sunset?'

Once again, I saw that excited boy way back on that first day at Roseworthy College with the world in front of him. His dreaming of a future had returned and we were both carried along with the moment. He was back to the Stephen we had known a few years ago. It had been a long time since we had seen him like this.

I agreed that the view of the sunset was magnificent, and the small units were in a perfect position for anyone interested in investing in tourism. He again brought up the subject of owning his own fruit property, adding to the conversation other ideas he'd thought of.

An Awkward Fit

As we drove to the hotel for our evening meal, Stephen chatted about some of the antics he and Wolly got up to. He grinned as he began his tale of the ill-fated roast.

One evening after work, the two boys decided to walk to the local hotel for a drink. It only took them ten minutes to walk the distance. Coming home, they passed some clubrooms where an irresistible aroma of roast meat caught their attention. A look each gave the other confirmed they were thinking the same thing. They hadn't had a roast for ages and curiosity got the better of them, so they followed their noses which led them to the back of the clubrooms where they came upon several Weber ovens. They lifted the lid on one and found two pieces of roast beef cooking, and guessed it was the same in the others. The club was obviously hosting a large group for dinner, and the car park was pretty full.

One of them commented that a roast like that would keep them in meat for a week. Being in a mad mood, Stephen grabbed one of the roasts and put it under his jumper and off they ran. A few metres down the road they saw a police car coming their way. They turned and walked in the opposite direction, but the car pulled up alongside them. Stephen quickly chucked the roast in the nearest front garden. After a friendly chat, with Stephen keeping his distance so the officers wouldn't detect the freshly cooked meat smell on his clothes, the police drove off. The boys retrieved their roast and took it home. They cut two slices off the meat, but felt so guilty they ended up giving the rest to the neighbour's dog that was always visiting them.

Our evening was off to a great start. We were still laughing as we got out of the car. I said something like 'Those poor people. I can just imagine the cook announcing, 'Sorry, everyone, but we are short of meat. Someone stole our roast beef.'

'Shhh! Quiet, Mum. I have to live here, and if anyone finds out, the whole town will know.'

Our fun continued. As we ate dinner, Stephen told jokes, and tried to pinch some prawns from Darrel's plate. Afterwards, we sat at the bar for a quiet drink.

Stephen bought me a small glass of something I was not familiar with, but he assured me I would like it. I took a polite sip and found it quite pleasant. Stephen whispered, 'Mum, you're supposed to skol it.'

So that's what I attempted to do. But not being in the habit of skolling drinks, I misfired. The liquid went flying out of the glass, past my open mouth and over my shoulder! Well, my poor son was aghast, but he recovered enough to say, 'I just won't tell anyone you're my mother.'

Darrel and I dropped Stephen off at his unit at about 9.30 pm. As we were preparing to say goodbye I remembered a message we had for him. 'Stephen, your mate Chris phoned us and asked us to tell you to telephone him.

He has something to ask you.' I said as he was getting out of the car.

'Okay,' he said 'Spose he wants me to move the rest of my gear out of his place.'

We both hugged him as we said our goodbyes, and then watched him disappear inside. Loneliness and trepidation swept over me, I was drawn in two directions. I didn't want to leave, but Darrel said, 'That's the best we've seen him for a long time; it looks like he's getting it together. He really appreciated us coming.'

'Yes, I think he's going to make it,' I agreed.

That evening, we drove the 20 minutes to Darrel's mother's house, where we spent the night. We headed home early next morning, happy in the knowledge that Stephen was confident and managing quite well.

Helen and Stephen's friend Megan Hickman (postscript)

Helen, Darrel with Stephen holding Ryan

Stephen in the Park with his nephew Ryan
(Picture found in his camera after he died)

The Pepper corn tree

Stephen on top of Uluru

Elaine and Tom Langrish from Devon in England

Helen and Darrel at Uluru

Part 4

CHAPTER 25 – 1998 - The incredible dream

Its Monday 3.51 am. I have just woken from a most incredible dream. I found myself running over grassy rolling hills with the wind in my hair on a warm sunny cloudless sky. As I reached the top of a hill, impulsively I threw myself into a dive. As I fell the wind caught me and lifted me into the air. I skimmed above ground about 20 feet high using my outstretched arms to keep my balance, landing 500 metres away on my feet.

The people knew I was strange among them, for they had an Indian way about them. It was like a reserve in modern times, 1980 – 1990's. They used modern technology to enhance the beauty and preserve the natural resources provided for them by the valley in which they lived. I dreamed the people who lived gentle lives discovered my gift of flight and revered me as one who was sent to them, to learn from them and them from me. They said I was once one of them and had become lost, but was now seeking my way home. Yet my home is caught in the past and lost in time. My gift was special and I should not reveal it to those who may try to harm me.

I tried jumping from a higher place and was taken into the sky many kilometres high so that I had a view of the whole valley and beyond. I started to fall as panic at being at such a height almost overcame me. It was all a case of balance. I had to stay lying flat and moving to keep the wind under me so I could glide.

The ruffians chased me. I ran to the hills and dived down the side of a hill to be lifted into the air and glide to safety. The dream, the place, and the people were so real, lasting

a couple of days (5 hours in real time). There's so much more to tell you but I work tomorrow.

~

Saturday 15 August was the last time we saw our son, Stephen alive.
On the evening of Sunday 16 August, Stephen drove from Barmera to Loxton to see his nana and return some egg cartons and jam jars. On his last visit, Ivy had stocked him up with eggs, soups and jams. We never left her place, after a visit, without our car boot full of food. It was a cold August night and it was dark by 5.30 pm so, with nothing else to do, she climbed into her warm bed and dozed. She heard a knock on the back door, but thinking it was one of the neighbours, she didn't answer. Stephen left the containers at the back door and returned home to Barmera.

Next day – Monday – was work as usual for Stephen. In the evening, he made a phone call to his mate, Chris, who had some exciting news – he and his partner were getting married in a fortnight and they wanted Stephen to be groomsman. Stephen was honoured and delighted to accept.
He missed his friends and longed to be back living in his Gawler unit, and working on his car. He described to Chris the incredible dream he had experienced the evening before. He couldn't stop thinking about it. He wondered what it meant.

Stephen's boss later confirmed that on Tuesday 18 August Stephen was at work as usual, showing no obvious concerns or any indication of what was to take place in the next 48 hours. That evening, after he had finished work and eaten dinner, Stephen dropped in at the neighbours' for a drink.

The neighbour recalls:

Stephen came to my unit. He had a two-litre cask of port wine and a glass with him. While there, he and I talked and drank wine. I think Stephen only had one glass. He stayed at my unit until about 9.45 pm before leaving.

At about 10 pm Stephen returned to my flat, with a bag of marijuana. He asked me if I wanted some. I told him 'No' and that I was going to bed. Stephen collected his wine and glass and left. That is the last time I saw him.

On Wednesday 19 August, I hadn't seen Stephen. His car, a green Holden station wagon, was still under his carport. A workmate of his came to his flat; I believe he didn't turn up for work. On Thursday, I still hadn't seen Stephen. I saw that his blinds were drawn and I became concerned for him. I phoned the police at about 12.30 pm.

While Stephen was at my flat, I would describe him as happy. He was slightly intoxicated, only to the stage that he was merry. He did not appear to be depressed at all. However, he was homesick. He was missing his family and friends and couldn't wait to go back and live in his Gawler unit.

On Thursday 20 August, after the police had been contacted, they obtained the key to Stephen's flat from the land agent and entered the unit at about 2 pm. Our son had hanged himself from an exposed timber rafter.

On searching the unit, police officers located a writing pad on the bed head.

This pad contained four pages of Stephen's handwriting. They also found one packet of Valium with only seven tablets left and one container of Haloperidol, both of which are antidepressants. Both are prescription drugs and had been purchased from the local chemist two weeks earlier.

They also found a half-smoked pipe containing burnt marijuana. Stephen's boss had previously been a police officer. He was called in to identify him, and the police notified us not long after on that same day.

Two days later, Darrel, Murray (our daughter's husband) and I travelled to Barmera to retrieve Stephen's belongings and drive his car back to Adelaide. When we entered the unit my eyes went immediately to the rafters, to find some evidence of what he had done.

Darrel had rung and warned the police that we were coming and asked them to remove any obvious signs. I needed to see something for confirmation. However, I did not expect to see what we saw. The rope was still tied to the window support and extended over the rafter, with about half a metre of rope hanging down. After getting over the initial shock at what he was looking at, Darrel removed the rope. It was difficult because Stephen had tied it with several knots very tightly. This confirmed that he really had done this to himself; it was reality.

We were traumatised. Time was standing still. The anxiety and dreadfulness of it all had not yet hit either of us. Deep inside me, a voice kept saying, 'Why aren't you crying? Why are you acting so strangely cool about it all?' I was in shock and the full reality of it hadn't yet reached me. The initial reaction and realisation that our only son was dead, when the policeman first told us on our front door, had passed. Now I was in a daze, going through the motions of collecting his belongings and tying up loose ends, while we waited for the autopsy to be carried out.

In one of the kitchen drawers in his Barmera unit, I discovered a receipt dated that Wednesday morning at 7.40 am. It was for a set of tyres fitted to his car, which bothered me, because it was the same day we were told he had died. Issues that would seem trivial, under normal circumstances, became a major disturbance for us and I became very confused. I was determined to retrace Stephen's movements leading up to the day he died.

The name of the attendant where he bought the tyres was on the receipt, and I phoned him from Adelaide. He remembered Stephen buying the tyres although he was not clear about the exact morning when they were bought. It was possible that the receipt hadn't been processed in the computer until the next day, which would mean they were purchased on the last day Stephen went to work. If that was the case, then it is very strange that, having already arranged to put the tyres on his boss's account until payday, when he arrived at work that morning he didn't mention the tyres, or that his boss didn't notice them.

I have to wonder also why he would go to the trouble of buying new tyres for his car if he had planned to kill himself. To a normal person, it doesn't make sense. The only answer is that once again that insidious, invasive illness had surfaced and, this time, he was unable to fight it.
The police had told Darrel that Stephen had been determined to take his life because he had used a knife to dig out the straw ceiling and part of the wooden rafter beam so that he could get the rope around it.

Even though the pathologist stated in his report there was no evidence of Stephen smoking marijuana prior to his suicide, I was not fully convinced, especially when it is remembered that Stephen had gone to his next-door neighbour on the Tuesday night to see if she wanted to have a joint with him.
I would like to pretend that Stephen didn't smoke marijuana at all. He was much too sensible to do that! But I need to face reality, however much my heart wants to deny it. I must tell the truth as I see it. Otherwise, how can I find answers to what happened to him, what went wrong, and how can this story help others?

To verify my concerns, I visited the local library. After reading several books, including *Drugs and Your Teenager* by Martin Palin, *The Parent's Complete Guide to Young People and Drugs* by James Kay and Julian Cohen, and *Kids + Drugs* by Paula Goodyear, I am convinced that, in all probability, Stephen would have consumed marijuana prior to his suicide. All the books I referred to in my research are in agreement that marijuana is detectable in the body up to seven days after the initial consumption. My mind is not at peace on this issue.

We also wonder if Stephen's death was linked with the general anaesthetic he received when his wisdom tooth was removed in hospital.

Upon further investigation, I found there are conflicting opinions about the effects of general anaesthetics on the level of serotonin in the brain, a brain chemical (neurotransmitter) that helps to regulate moods .A lack of it can lead to depression.

I contacted the dental surgeon and the anaesthetist, asking for information about the procedure that was carried out. I soon discovered that opinions on this subject varied. One lead I was given was the name of a professor at the Royal Adelaide Hospital who lectured on the effects of anaesthetic. According to him, there is no evidence of anaesthetic affecting the serotonin level in the brain, causing a chemical imbalance and resulting in feelings of anxiety and depression. He said that depression from having surgery would more likely be caused from pain, and possibly from other drugs required after certain operations.

Since then, Darrel has had major sinus surgery. Six weeks later, he asked the operating specialist, 'Why do I feel very depressed? I try to hide it, but I get aggravated, short-tempered, and feel snappy. I feel people are in my face and I just want to be left alone.'

The specialist replied, 'My God! What else would you expect after such major surgery?' He went on to talk about the effect on the brain due to the close proximity of where the operation was performed. He also explained, at great length, the chemical imbalance called serotonin in Darrel's brain.

The effect on the serotonin level causes people to feel depressed and tired. He offered Darrel antidepressants, which he turned down, saying he would fight it. The specialist said quite specifically that anaesthetic would make you feel depressed. Darrel's firsthand experience and the fact that Stephen, who was psychologically impaired, had also had an operation in the same general area, raised questions in my mind. Surely if Darrel, who has never suffered depression in the past, had this outcome from his operation, wouldn't a person with Stephen's difficulties be open to suffering the same problems?

I was looking for answers. I turned to the medication Stephen had been taking and I searched the Internet. Copious information about these drugs was available, but not having a medical background made it very difficult for me to fully understand it. However, I discovered a warning that Haloperidol will add to the effects of alcohol and other drugs that affect the central nervous system, which would have included the Valium. I also read that patients taking these medications should check with their doctor or dentist before undergoing an anaesthetic.

I believe it was an explosive cocktail of the above factors that caused Stephen – even if only for a short time – to feel confused and desperate enough to want to end his life.

The police presumed that the hand written pages on Stephen's bed head were all written at the same time. However, on studying them more closely, I found the first three were an explanation of a dream he'd had on the Sunday night that he couldn't get out of his mind, which he'd told his mate Chris about when he rang him on the Monday night.

CHAPTER 26 – 1998 - The agony and grief

Today I realise what the dream meant. The events in the dream were representative of the real world way of things. I am a genius but wish not to be used. I see so clearly I'm an emotional wreck, so I cannot deal with stressful situations. I don't have all the answers *but* I'm very good at finding solutions and have learnt great patience.
I don't write much these days and I'm not worried about neatness, I am writing this on my knee!
I don't mean to have hurt anyone; I just can't live with the torment of an overactive mind, which makes me eventually become physically drained. Believe me, I love life but I have to rest now! Love to all my friends, family, Linda and Kailah.

This was Stephen's last piece of writing, his last words.

~

We couldn't hold a funeral service for Stephen until after the autopsy.

Life became totally consumed by grief. I felt as if I was on a stage and forced to perform. I concentrated on what was happening around me, not wanting to let my thoughts go beyond the existence of everyday life. There would be time later to dwell on the past and look for answers. For now, I focused on the constant stream of visitors and the phone calls. The rest of life didn't exist.

Pastor Alan Schreiber and his wife from our church came around to talk and help us make funeral arrangements. I insisted I didn't need my sister, Jan, to stay and help. She didn't listen to me and stayed, anyway. She washed the endless pile of dishes caused by the endless flow of people drinking the tea and coffee she made for them.

Sometimes, I crept into my bedroom or curled up in some small corner where my heart gave way to the indescribable pain and sorrow. I tried to rock my grief away. It helped a little.

The autopsy results came back. The toxicology report revealed Stephen had .053 alcohol in his blood but no trace of any other drugs. Because we knew he sometimes used marijuana, we were sure he would have had some in his system. The fact that there was a bag of it in his unit, as well as the half-smoked pipe, and the fact that he'd asked his neighbour to share some with him, were telling factors. Darrel and I requested for the test to be done again, but the same results came back. We do not feel convinced that these results are correct. On the morning of Wednesday 26 August 1998, Darrel, Nicky and I went to see Stephen before the funeral service.

Difficult as it is to write this, it is therapeutic because these memories and feelings have been buried inside me for so long. And so many times, I've gone over this in my mind, wondering whether we could have conducted any differently that very special and final time we spent together as a family.

As we approached Stephen, each step became heavier. I wanted to be with him, yet I didn't want this moment to arrive. Death was about to become a reality. I felt alone and empty. I don't remember any of us speaking, yet I wanted to say so much to him. It was too late. I stroked his forehead and reshaped his hair the way he always wore it. I didn't want to leave him alone in this cold place, but I had to. I felt that I was being forced to bury him, going against anything I wished to happen. I had to go home and get dressed for his funeral, where we would say goodbye to him with his friends and the rest of the family. That afternoon, before the service, we again had a viewing time, inviting our friends to say goodbye to Stephen before we went into church.

Nicole and I were with him. Darrel was in the church, making sure the sound system worked properly to play Stephen's favourite song. Darrel greeted our friends and relatives. *I couldn't – wouldn't – leave our son.* Nicole cried and said, 'I'm so sorry, Mum.'

'Come and say goodbye to our son. He's out the back,' was how Darrel greeted those waiting for the service to start. He took them around the back to where we were with Stephen.

As I saw how much Stephen was loved and admired, an overwhelming pride in our son stirred deep within me. People attended whom I didn't even know. So, too, were friends we had known from many years ago and with whom we had lost touch. It helped enormously to see all these caring people who came to say goodbye and support us.

Some approached the room cautiously and hung around, not sure if they should come in. 'It's okay, it's okay!' (it bloody well wasn't okay.) *Wake up! – wake up!* I repeated silently over and over, as the tears quietly rolled down my face.

I kept soothing Stephen's forehead, more for me than for him. Those sad, grieving friends who were still in shock came slowly forward. Words were useless; no one spoke. I kept looking at our son. I would hold this picture in my mind forever. I didn't want to lose one moment, knowing this would be the last time I would see him.

I stood, taking in every detail – the way his hands were placed, even his fingernails; I read the words in his face. *It doesn't matter any more, it's all over.*

I became aware of two very special people who were still in mourning for their own son, Kym. That very morning, Kym's father had been reading the paper during his morning break at work when he did something he hadn't done since his son's death – he read the funeral notices. He said that, for some unknown reason, he was compelled to look this day. He was unaware of Stephen's death until he saw the funeral notice for that afternoon.

He rang his wife and said, 'Get dressed, we are going to a funeral this afternoon,' and told her what he had read. They had come to support us.

Darrel finally joined Nicole and me in the small outer room while the guests were filling up the church. 'It's time to go,' the attendants said, several times. 'It's getting late. We don't want to rush you, but we have booked a time for the cemetery.'

We dragged ourselves away, but we didn't want to leave Stephen. As we walked through the door, Darrel stopped and went back in as the men were reaching for the lid. 'Wait, I'll do that. I saw him into the world, I will see him out.' He put the lid on and screwed it down.

Everyone was seated; listening to *Love is a bridge that goes from heart to heart*, one of Stephen's favourite songs he often played on his guitar when he was younger. Nicky, together with Murray, Darrel and me, walked down the aisle with Stephen's coffin being wheeled in behind us.

We had asked Stephen's mate, Chris, to say a few words at the service. As I listened carefully, I was able to get to know another side to our son. I hung onto every word.

Chris said:

We shouldn't be mourning a death; we celebrate a life. I'm standing here as a favour for a mate. Steve's life was as full as a person's life could possibly be. I met Steve through friends.

He was a great bloke; we both played bass guitar and he invited me around to his place. I couldn't believe what I saw. He had his computer spread all over the floor. I had never seen anything like it before. He had it together in about ten minutes and we were playing a game with it. That blew me away. It was the same dedication to everything he had, to every goal he set. Steve's life was full on.

The one thing I can say is his heart was pure; nothing he did was for himself.

He invited me and the missus around to a fondue night. I had never been to a fondue before; he said 'It's really good fun.' We were vegetarians. I rolled around and his whole lounge had been cleared out.

There was a whole mountain of food and we ate and ate for about three hours. That was the generosity that Steve gave to his friends. I can't say how many times he helped me out; he was always there when I needed someone. He loved to talk and I loved to listen to him talk, and he listened in the same way to me. I was glad to have his advice and encouragement.

I can't believe the athleticism of the bloke. He rode to Blanchetown and back on his pushbike, got back about two in the morning. We were having a party and he came. Later that morning, he went to the beach with us, and so I'm thinking this guy's full on. We swam out and decided to go to the jetty. We got halfway and I said,

'How are you going, Steve?' He said, 'Yeah, not too bad, but I can't go on.' And he just went straight down. I mean, he had just ridden more than 200 kilometres, come straight to our party and now was swimming. I swam over and up popped his head. A boat was going past and we waved it down and he took us back to shore. I could go on and on. But to wrap it up I want to say Steve was just a pure, pure man. Everything he did had meaning and giving to someone else.

I would do it ten times over. Steve, keep looking down on me, mate, we all love you.

Chris then closed with a reading from the Bible, Psalm121: 1&2.

I look to the mountains;
where will my help come from?
My help will come from the Lord,
who made heaven and earth.

The events of that day are extraordinarily vivid. Even the weather, my hairstyle, where we stood.

For Darrel, Nicky, Stephen and me it was the saddest, but most beautiful, closest union a family could have. Love was powerful, like a spirit moving between us, gathering all our love together and sending it with Steve as we lowered him into the grave.

'Bye, son', were Darrel's last words to him. Stephen was still at last, and released from all the horror he had suffered. But this should never have been the way to end his suffering and pain.

Where was the help?

Most of the guests were barely recognisable shapes; it was our small but very close family unit that was the centre of my world that day. Darrel's only brother was at home at our house, too sick to be with us.

He had travelled on the bus from Mildura but wasn't fit enough to make the funeral. His wife Sadie was there, but she was grieving for her sister, whose body was one of those only recently dug up from a back yard in Salisbury North, linked to the murders in Snowtown.

About 200 people attended the funeral, held at the Elizabeth Lutheran Church. We buried our only son that winter's day in a white coffin at the Smithfield native bush cemetery, about a 10 minute drive from where he spent the major part of his life.

The Snowtown killings in South Australia were uncovered in 1999. Ten people were murdered in Australia's biggest serial killing.

CHAPTER 27 – 1998 - The peppercorn tree

After the funeral there was nothing but emptiness; all that was left was an agonising silence. The door to life had shut for Stephen and I was devoid of anything but a deep, deep unhappiness. Before long, the full realisation of what had happened hit me. Each moment was agony. How could such misery and heartache exist? I could not plan the future. I felt as if my heart had been ripped out. I wanted to die. I faced an almost impossible journey ahead of me.

How will I survive?

I found myself imitating Stephen and doing the things he liked to do. I spent long hours on the computer and in the library, looking up information on schizophrenia, psychological illnesses, death, and suicide.

I searched for pictures of figures hanging from the end of a rope. I read, and then read again, science fiction novels, books about death and dying, what happens after death, descriptions of how one can hang oneself successfully. It sounds crazy, but I had lost my identity and, in some ways, took on my son's, wanting to feel how I imagined he felt. I tormented myself. It was almost as if I was doing his living for him. I spent endless hours researching and typing out my soulful reflections on his computer, actions that mimicked his behaviour in life. It was Stephen – he was still living in me. I was keeping him alive for just that little bit longer. This was the only way I could bear living.

I went to church a couple of times, but I felt uncomfortable, as though I didn't belong there any more. Each time they sang, I cried. I didn't want to hear about God. Every time I even thought about God, I had to think of Stephen and I couldn't bear putting the two together.

As the days became weeks, I realised how much life had changed. I was different – full of anger and pain. Darrel and I were unable to find words to comfort each other.

Day after day, my anger surfaced. I would explode, look around for something to throw, and then dissolve into tears. I fought to stay calm.

Why couldn't I have helped him more? What did I do wrong? Why couldn't I save him?

I seethed, I was so angry with Stephen for doing this to me, so angry with Darrel; everything about Darrel made me even more angry. My anger showed in my body language and the way I spoke. I took to swearing;

'f….f…..f…' became my favourite saying. I was so angry; I was like a time bomb waiting to explode at the slightest thing. Darrel couldn't understand me. I couldn't understand me. I had been completely and utterly transformed. Darrel didn't reproach me. He suffered my anger silently. Even though he was grieving and hurting as much as I was, he was exceedingly patient with the abuse that came his way.

We were warned by others going through the same grief of losing a child to watch our marriage. Many had failed under such circumstances and I could understand why. If Darrel had not been as patient and had retaliated, it would have given me reason, in my mind, to leave him, because that is what I wanted to do. I wanted to escape from anything that reminded me of Stephen. I was selfish; but then grief is selfish, it is totally personal.

We needed help to work through our grief. Telstra, where Darrel worked, gave us the name of a counselling service. Darrel made an appointment, stressing that we wanted someone who had experience working with those left behind after suicide.

When we arrived for our appointment, we were met by someone who had only dealt with children. Darrel lost control and exploded, 'you're no bloody good to us.' He held my arm and steered me out the door.

We never went back. It didn't help that we had just come from a meeting at the Coroner's Office to go through the results of the autopsy, and were feeling fragile and shaken. It was at this point that Darrel seemed to close up. He no longer had a son; that bond had been severed.

There would be no more fishing trips, quiet chats or outings together. He seemed to crawl into a dark cave to protect himself from the hurt and to let the world go by until he was ready to emerge. I tried to get him to respond but he was afraid of adding to my pain, so each of us grieved alone in our own way. In the first few weeks, Nicky tried to give me support, but I knew I would drag her down with me, so I said I would be okay. Having been through losing my own brother, I knew her pain. I also knew her children would be her strength. They needed her and she would cope, even if it was difficult.

The door to my life had closed. I couldn't see beauty in anything. I looked at the gum trees that only a short time ago had seemed so full of grace and splendour – they meant nothing to me, I hated looking at them. It was not just happiness that eluded me; the will to live had gone. This world meant nothing to me, I hated it, hated the unspeakable pain I was going through. *Was I going crazy?* Yes, I was losing control over everything, my thoughts, and my body. Helplessness overwhelmed me. The dark shadow of death consumed everything that had existed for me. It had taken my son, leaving me behind, still in its grip.

With so much time on my hands I took to writing down my feelings. This seemed about the only thing over which I had any control. I was too devastated to do anything else. As Stephen's death was self-inflicted, it brought additional stress and with that came many questions and much self-doubt. I couldn't face going out so I became isolated and I had neither energy nor willpower to cope with housework or cooking. More often than not, I waited for Darrel to come home from work to help me cook dinner. I had a complete indifference to life. I felt it didn't really matter if I died. I wanted so much to be with my son. But, despite willing myself to die, I knew I couldn't, because I had a husband and a daughter who needed me. Nevertheless, I withdrew from the world. I couldn't be with people or tolerate their contentment, when all I could see was sadness.

I tried again to find someone suitable to confide in. I felt few options were available to me. I made an appointment to see a Lutheran minister, Pastor Andy Kowald in Nuriootpa, who was patient and kind and let me pour out my grief. Talking to him opened up a whole new world of difficult questions I hadn't thought of before. It also put a different perspective on many things – thoughts I had pushed into the background and had not fully resolved. Amazingly, amidst the confusion of it all, I began slowly feeling a little more positive, although a sense of guilt hung over me. I blamed myself for not knowing how to fix my son's illness.

Six months before Stephen died, I was waiting in the doctor's surgery to see a specialist. The patient before me came out and spoke to the receptionist, his voice quiet and sad. It was the accent and tone of his voice that made me take notice. I recognised him as a gymnastics coach at Nicky's club. His name was Spiro. His son, Julio, had also been a coach and Nicky's friend. Julio often visited Nicole when she was still living at home, to work out gymnastic routines for the boys of the club.

Spiro was telling the receptionist that his son had recently committed suicide and that life was very difficult for him. I remember that when this happened Nicky was very upset. She went to his funeral but she asked me not to tell Stephen about this, which indicates that she also feared for his safety.

At that time, I wanted to approach Spiro to express my regret about his son, but I knew he hadn't recognised me as Nicky's mother so I decided against it. Six months later, I was to suffer the same fate.

I learned that Julio, who was 24 years old, was buried in direct line with Stephen, two rows over. A week later, I again saw Spiro at our local shopping centre, and this time I introduced myself as Nicky's mother and told him of our tragedy. I could feel the wave of despair washing over him. He immediately wanted to contact Nicky. Since then, when either Darrel and I or Spiro and his wife visit the cemetery, we take a little time to put a flower on the other son's headstone, in a moment of reflection and compassion.

This unusual connection continued to include the coming together of more of us who were left behind. We had noticed a headstone a short distance from our son's, also in the same row as Julio. A young man named Michael had died the same year as Stephen and probably within a week or so. Both were around the same age. There was no specific date on the headstone, only July 1998. We eventually ran into the father, when we were visiting the cemetery one Sunday, and struck up a conversation. He, like Darrel was from a Polish background. Michael's father and brother had discovered his body when they went to visit him in his flat in Adelaide. He was 26 years old, had been suffering from schizophrenia and taken his life with drugs.

I then met another family whose daughter had died two years after Stephen, in April 2000. She was 30 years old, and the young daughter discovered her mother's body hanging in their back veranda one morning when getting ready for school.

This young woman would have known Stephen – they went to the same high school .*Was it fate that brought these young*

people together in death, whose lives were intertwined? What are the chances of this happening?
Now, visiting the graveside of our children has brought some solace to us, as parents, knowing we are not alone in what we are going through.

I read Stephen's desperate writings over and over until they became imprinted on my mind. His words showed me the magnitude of his despair, and I knew these pages held something rare. How many records of the innermost thoughts and workings of the mind of a psychologically ill person exist? *I could almost hear him telling me to let others know how he felt, so that he could be understood. I wanted to do this for him.*

For a while, that wonderful God-given gift of thought and creativity eluded me. Each time I tried to put something down on paper, I was gripped by grief taking hold and fighting against me. I was defenceless. I had no power to fight against it and, as I sunk into deep depression and anxiety, I repeated over and over: '*I can't do this!*' I would leave it for a month, then return to the computer and try again. I tried to force myself, but reading Stephen's words tore me apart. I was in utter despair; I had never written a story or a poem in my life. I wasn't even a *reader.*
But this thought would not leave me. I became obsessed with it. Suddenly, I felt old. I had reached the bottom of the pit of sadness; life was shit.
I'm so alone. How can my heart keep on beating when it is in so much pain? Give me back my son. Restore his life. Let him come home.
How could I not have saved him? Am I so dumb and stupid that I couldn't find the answer? No, now I am kidding myself. I am still denying his mental condition.

I have returned to work for two half days a week. I barely survive without breaking down with the agony I am experiencing. At the end of my shift, I can't wait to leave. The short distance to where the car is parked seems so far away. My chest feels so tight and my stomach is in spasms.

How can this be happening? My body's not going to survive. I've got to release this pain before I explode.

I am in the car driving home and I can no longer hold this anguish inside me. The screams come over and over and the tears roll down my face. I can hardly see where I am driving. God, I wish I could die! This is unbearable! I can't take any more!

Why was he born? Why was I born? Neither of us should have existed. It was a cruel trick that the devil played. What a f... rotten game to play. I don't want to play any more. Let me go. Let me die.

My mind started to play tricks on me. I was seeing visions of Stephen with his arms out to me, willing me to join him.

As the months passed, I became aware of gradual, small changes taking place. I was getting out into the community a bit more, although I realised that there were other challenges I had to face that would destroy my composure. One such occasion was an appointment with a gynaecologist. The one I usually saw for my annual examination had retired. This was my first appointment with the new one and it required him taking some medical history. He began with general questions about my family background but, knowing where this was heading, I began to panic as I tried to think of an answer to the as-yet-unasked question. And then it came: 'How many children do you have?'

Tears streamed down my face as I sobbed, uncontrollably. Finally, I dried my eyes and regained my composure enough to say, 'I'm sorry. I had two children; my son suicided not long ago.'

It was then my turn to be surprised, as this very professional, gently spoken man began to cry.

Within seconds he was composed again and said, 'Please forgive me. It was the shock. I lost my son in the same way. 'Although we never spoke of it again, a special understanding developed between us and I felt his compassion for me on each return visit.

It took me a long time to work out how to respond to people who asked how many children I had. We raised a son and daughter and nothing can take that fact away. Someone who existed will always be there. My mind cannot comprehend ignoring the existence of one of my children.

For about the first year after Stephen died, I used to say, 'I have two children but our son is not with us any more; he passed away.' But then, as I felt better, I was able to say, 'I have a daughter,' and let them decipher things as they wished.

While writing this book, I was able to chart my progress from my jottings on the computer. Eighteen months were to pass after Stephen's death before I began to *want* to live again. I wanted to change, do something different to fill the gaping hole in my life. There would always be a place in my heart where Stephen belongs, but I still wanted to live and desperately wanted not to hurt so much.

While I can now see the advances I was making, at the time it seemed slow. I would take one step forward, then two steps back. I was missing Stephen terribly and could do nothing about it. I started getting anxiety attacks. A deep anguish would engulf me without warning. I would become short of breath and my chest would hurt as if my body was trying to release all my pent-up anger.

'What a shit of a way to be,' I wrote on the computer. I decided to do something about it and went to my doctor.

'There is no pill for grief,' she said. 'I could give you something to make you feel better but it will just delay the grief.' She told me to take up walking, and suggested that exercise was the best way I could help myself.

I did this. It helped a little.

An Awkward Fit

I continued to read Stephen's writings. I was more determined than ever to put them into a book. The book was becoming an obsession. I couldn't put it out of my mind. By now, I was thinking it could be of help to others to know what Stephen was feeling and thinking, and knowing what difficulties he had come up against.

As I began writing, I struck the same problem as before. It was too painful and took up so much of my energy that I would feel devastated and have to leave it alone for a while. I persisted though and little by little, the book started to take shape.

By now, it was into the second year without my son and, for most of the time, I was able to control my grief. Still, never a day went by without Stephen being constantly on my mind. Often, I visualised him lying in the coffin and would break down, but by now I was able to shake myself out of it. Life was a chore, really hard work, and I was often very emotional and teary.

It was at this time I felt I had to get away; I wanted to disappear. Darrel supported my decision to return alone to Poland. It was May 2000, nearly two years since Stephen died. I chose Poland because of its distance and because our friends over there could not speak English and our conversations would be limited, revolving around the smattering of 'survival Polish' I had learnt. This was the best thing I could have done because it took me totally away from the world I was living in, a world I didn't want to be in.

Our friends in Poland were aware of my loss and were very kind to me. I was able to put Stephen out of my mind most of the time because I needed all of my concentration to find the right words to be able to communicate. I had a wonderful time. It was as if I had entered another world entirely and home didn't exist.

From Poland, I went to England. Stephen had promised Tom and Elaine that he would visit them two years after our outback holiday, and I wanted to make this trip for him. It was part of my healing, too. However, it was a hard trip and emotionally draining, as I felt Stephen's presence everywhere. I felt, though, that this was a turning point for me. I had fulfilled Stephen's promise to Elaine and Tom, and I knew we would remain close friends.

Over the next year – three years after Stephen's death – I continued to struggle with my grief, though I felt I was getting better and more able to get on with my life with reasonable calm. But these feelings of renewed vigour didn't last for long as the anxiety attacks returned. I was now working as an assistant in a speech and language program within a kindergarten. Feelings of insecurity returned, too, and I had to fight and resist them. My confidence in driving the car was much improved, although I had the odd relapse.

On one occasion, I was returning home from the Golden Grove shopping centre, totally frustrated. The feeling had started the previous evening when I'd tried to master the complexities of Internet banking, to no avail. So, after work this day, I stopped off at the bank.

On the way home, a horrible wave of anxiety washed over me. Every nerve and muscle in my face ached and my stomach was in knots. Tears rolled down my face, out of control. I glanced to my left and the road gave way to a ravine full of gum trees. It crossed my mind how easy it would be to veer off the road into the hollow. That thought lasted only a split second, but it scared me enough to visit my doctor.

This time, the doctor thought I had been struggling with grief for long enough on my own, and that perhaps I needed some help to rediscover the feeling of normality. She prescribed a low dose of antidepressants. Those feelings of anxiety and self-destruction stopped and I felt better able to cope. This meant I was able to spend more time on the book and, although it continued to upset me rehashing painful experiences, I continued with it.

Darrel accepted my need to write the book. He couldn't get involved in it, though, because it brought too many painful memories to the surface that he'd managed to bury. However, he was very supportive of me and accepted the many nights and very early mornings when I sat for hours typing out my thoughts. He even cooked dinner if I was busy writing, although he would make sure that I didn't overdo it.

Since Stephen ended his life, it has been difficult for us. Grief has been merciless. We have needed to continue to function, in order to cope. Darrel and I decided to go fishing when we were in Loxton visiting Mum Mac and helping her sort out her paperwork. We found a nice quiet spot along the riverbank, not far from where a young family of five were swimming.

Bronte, our dog, was with us and we took him for a short swim first. Afterwards, I sat on a clump of couch grass near the water's edge while Darrel set up his fishing lines. Bronte was on a lead and I looped the end around my ankle so he wouldn't roll in the dirt.

As a family, we had spent a lot of time at the river. We swam, fished, camped and caught yabbies. I watched the sun across the water, trying to hide behind the tall gum trees that lined the opposite bank. I visualised Stephen, standing tall with a gum tree either side of him and the red and orange glow of the setting sun as a backdrop. He looked across at me and forced a smile on his troubled face.

Not much water flowed into the Murray river because of the drought and there was scarcely a movement in the water. Pelicans drifted gently along with the slightest movement of the current, plunging their bills below the surface from time to time looking for fish – there were five.

'Are you happy?' asked Darrel. He obviously was. He was only a couple of metres away, excitedly untangling the small callop he'd just caught.

I didn't shift my gaze from across the water as I replied, 'I'm calm.'

It was an honest response. I was enjoying being back where we had spent so much time together; it felt peaceful and comfortable. *But happy?* I am happy sometimes, when I'm not thinking about it, and I am enjoying more of my life as time goes on. But I can't think of 'happy' without Stephen coming into my mind, and then I become sad.

As we drove away from Loxton, I longed for my past life – a life with no shattered dreams. That night, I was restless and couldn't sleep. My feelings and thoughts were all of Stephen. At 1.30 am, I crept out of bed and wrote:

I see your vision, standing tall across the water,
You frown, and pretend to smile.
You never will grow old.
I'm glad you didn't cut your hair,
As you said you nearly did the last time we saw you.
You used to help us catch the fish;
We sat together, your dad and I,
Casting our lines into the water.
You loved it just like we do, just like this,
When the evening is warm and the sun is setting
And the pelicans are coasting along on the water.
Do you remember one time when we were together?
The pelican swallowed the fish you were reeling in?
We laughed.
But then you weren't impressed when you had to cut your line.
I bet you wished you could wring its neck,
Or at least pull out its feathers one by one.
What we have lost will never be returned;
We must live with this and hopefully learn from it.

I ask myself 'What went wrong? Why did this happen? Why couldn't I have done more to help him? Why didn't I see it coming? When did it all start going wrong? Were his differences and his communication difficulties part of the reason or all the cause of his problems? Was it the choices he made for himself? Was it something ever-present throughout his life, or just the latter part of it? And what about Roseworthy College – was that where it all began, when he moved away from home and was forced into an environment that was alien to him? What made him so complex? Was it his busy brain that never found its niche in life?'
So many questions. So few answers.

When Stephen said he didn't want us involved with his visits to the psychiatrist, I should have talked more about it and made him realise that I wanted to be involved, to share his problem and help with his healing. When I think back on this, I can see I was afraid of making him angry, of being rejected if I insisted on him letting us become involved. But the reality is that professional services are not allowed to enlighten parents as to the true nature of the illness of adult children unless the children themselves want that to happen.

Even now, I feel angry that we were kept in the dark. Stephen told his psychiatrist that we were the only people he could talk to and trust, so why didn't Stephen let us become involved? There are still odd days now when life gets too much for me to handle. I feel anxious and depressed and wish I could disappear. It's on those days that I feel that everything is crowding in on me. But those days don't come very often, and when I remember that after Stephen died *every* day consisted of these feelings, I can cope with the occasional bad day. I know there will always be days when something or someone triggers a memory that sets off my tears, but I can accept this. I don't think we will ever get over it, so it's a matter of learning to live with it.

However, when I look back, I can see the road to recovery that we've all travelled. For me, it has been learning to adjust to a world without my son. Life is different. Many things have changed since he was here. Our house has been renovated and we have a different car. Nicky now has twin boys and she and her family live in a different house. There are not so many reminders now, and I want it this way. I want to keep our past life as something we shared with Stephen, and this life as one that is different.

There are times when I still get depressed and the bleakness of it all floods over me. On these days, I withdraw from the world until the feeling passes, which it usually does by the next day. Mostly, though, I feel almost normal again. At least, I hope I am! It was only recently that I could bring myself to look more closely at the suicide note Stephen left. He didn't end his life because he hated it; he loved life.

He just couldn't cope with the crazy things that were going on in his mind.

The 'busy mind' is our family legacy; we inherited a problem-solving and creative mind. I can't imagine what it was like for Stephen, not being able to 'switch off,' and having a multitude of ideas and problems constantly congesting his thought patterns. He seemed to be a victim of his own thoughts and conscience. His suicided while the balance of his mind was temporarily imbalanced. Is he to blame for the despair that overtook him?

How do I feel now? I'm okay. I think I am dealing with it and coping.

The only thing is that I have forgotten how to be happy. I used to laugh a lot but I don't know how to laugh any more. I am going to have to teach myself to have fun and laugh again.

Losing Stephen left me with the feeling of having a responsibility to make my life different and more productive. This book will keep his memory alive but, more than that, I hope his writings and story will be of help to others suffering the same torments as him. Working through my own grief in the writing of this story has been a bonus. Not all of my questions are answered, but I did as much research as I needed to – for me – without raising deeper issues that I was not prepared to face.

Helen Maczkowiack

Final Words

The years have passed quickly. I finished the first draft of this book at the end of the third anniversary of Stephen's death. Another three years and three drafts later have passed and it is six years on, and during these last two years I have added bits and pieces and written the final chapter. Now I want to add my last piece.

I am busy in my life. I have several projects 'on the-go.' I still get angry or upset very easily, but I am stronger and more acutely aware of my sensitivities. I have a much greater awareness of my very intricate mind, the complexities of the brain, how it functions and how it shapes my world and, at times, how it has the ability to take over my life.

Sometimes I feel quiet and relaxed and go about my living quite calmly, but there are days when it feels like my mind comes alive and makes decisions for me and I can choose to let it take over or I can fight it.
I have one part of my grieving that I have discovered I am ready to work at.

I still feel the emptiness, I hear the hollow laughter echo inside me, I feel the smile often still needing to be forced – I need to learn how to really laugh and smile again and be genuinely happy. I can preserve my son Stephen's story in this book, I will have recorded his life, but the reality is ... he is not coming back I must face this and get on with life.

I wish I could have contributed more to finding peace for Stephen. When he died and we were removing his belongings from the unit, we came across the pot plant that I had thought was a marijuana plant and had hidden behind the shed. I brought it home. It has turned out to be a peppercorn tree, which now takes pride of place on our front veranda. It's very special, a little part of Steve that's still with me. As it grows bigger and stronger, it marks the passing of time, a reminder of how much stronger I am today than when I brought it home.

Postscript

By Megan Hickman

It was 2004, and I had started working for the Early Learning Programme, which is a home based program where our team of six workers visit the homes of children 0 to 5 who have learning difficulties, supporting the parents to help their children with their learning. I am the Aboriginal worker in the Salisbury district. Helen started the same day as an early learning field worker in the Kumangka Para district, and there was Pauline and Dolly also working for the Kumangka Para team and Gai, Jill and me for Salisbury. Pauline, Dolly and I dropped Helen home from work one day and she invited us in for coffee.

I had just entered the front hallway when I saw a picture of this guy on the hall table. He was immediately familiar. 'Is this your son?' I asked Helen.
She said he was so I asked what school he went to. 'Fremont High,' said Helen.
'No!' I insisted, 'No he didn't, what school did he go to?'
'*Oh!* He also went to Urrbrae in …'
'That's it – that's where he went! That's Stephen, that's my buddy.' I couldn't believe it! I was standing in the hallway of his mum's house and I had not connected the surnames – it was the photo that did it.

'He died six years ago,' said Helen.
I was stunned; I couldn't believe this was happening.
Stephen was my mate. He always raced to the last bus, the one I used to catch; it was the bus to the city. He always had the guitar with him because he was playing it every day. I had friends but no real friends. He looked like my brother-in-law, and he was tall and blond and sort of quiet. We were mates. We used to hang out in the music room and he always played

An Awkward Fit

Stairway to Heaven. Stephen didn't really know how good he was and we didn't always appreciate him, but that's life. Helen I can't believe he is your son and the way we found out. It was freaky.

Dolly was meant to be with me in the house that day. I felt extremely upset but Dolly made me look on it as a positive. The cycle came back round; I have made a connection with Stephen's spirit through his mum Helen.

I was in year 9 when Steve was there and he was year 10. I went off the rails in year 10. He was my mate when no-one else would be. I didn't belong. I knew I was different even when I was little, and mentally I thought I was like my step dad because he had the dark hair and Dad wanted to adopt a Nunga kid and that made him my dad because he wanted me.

Steve was my mate. Whether the friendship developed because of the loneliness of being different I don't know. Even now I have to tell myself to keep strong. Us blackfellas say the mind is a powerful thing; we shouldn't be taking drugs, etc, because we cannot let them take over our minds. If Stephen knew me now he would be proud.

Where to go for help

Lifeline Australia
Freecall: 13 11 14
www.lifeline.org.au
Lifeline International
Free call: 1300 13 11 14
www.lifeline.web.za
Mensline Australia
Phone: 1300 78 99 78
www.menslineaus.org.au
A counselling line for family relationship help.
Kids Help Line
Freecall. 1800 55 1800
www.kidshelp.com.au
A confidential telephone counselling service for children and young people in
Australia.
SANE helpline
Freecall: 1800 18 SANE (7263)
www.sane.org
Reach Out (Online service for young people)
www.reachout.com.au
Suicide Prevention Australia
www.suicidepreventionaust.org
DepressioNet
www.depressionet.com.au
For information and help to access professionals and treatment throughout
Australia.
Asperger Syndrome Australian Information Centre
http://members.ozemail.com.au/~rbmitch/Asperger.htm
An online support service for those involved with Asperger Syndrome in Australia.
EUFAMI ivzw (European Federation of Associations of Families of People with
Mental Illness) www.eufami.org

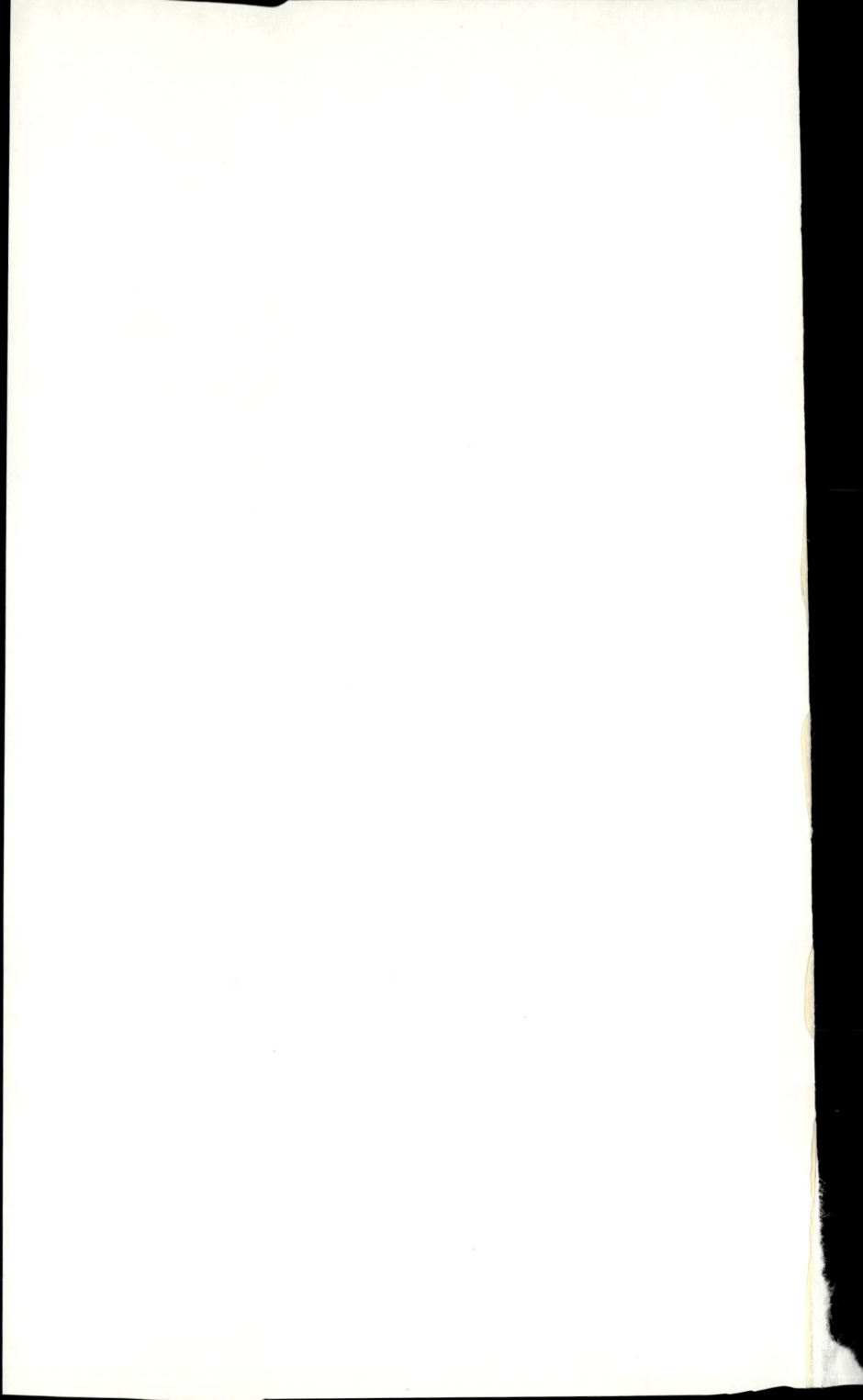